Gleanings from the Records of ZEPHANIAH JOB of Polperro

By

Frank H. Perrycoste

ISBN 978-09553648-2-2
ISBN 09553648-2-5

Published by
Polperro Heritage Press,
Clifton-upon-Teme, Worcestershire WR6 6EN
United Kingdom
www.polperropress.co.uk

Printed by
Orphans Press
Leominster
Herefordshire
United Kingdom

Introduction

Frank Hill Perrycoste and his artist wife Maud came to live in Polperro shortly after their marriage in 1898. Within a few years, he had embarked on an ambitious project to fingerprint the entire population of his adopted Cornish fishing village in order to provide material for Sir Francis Galton, the scientist who pioneered the study of fingerprints. The object of the experiment was to determine whether or not fingerprints were an inherited characteristic. To chart the relationships of the various individuals whose prints he obtained, Perrycoste also compiled pedigrees of the families concerned. Today these provide a rich source of information for genealogists.

Frank Perrycoste also developed a keen interest in local history and in the 1920s he was shown a large accumulation of papers, ledgers and letterbooks stored at Crumplehorn Mill that had once belonged to Zephaniah Job, the 'Smugglers' Banker' who financed the smuggling and privateering trade that flourished in Polperro in the late 18th and early 19th centuries. Despite the 'huge bonfire' that destroyed many of Job's records after his death in 1821, there was still 'half a hundred-weight of account books and debris'.

Perrycoste spent the last remaining years of his life, before his death in October 1930, sifting through the huge pile of books, ledgers and papers left by Job. His *Gleanings from the Records of Zephaniah Job of Polperro* was originally published in the *Cornish Times* in 1929 and later reprinted in a limited edition book that is now rare and long out of print.

This new edition contains a few footnotes to aid modern readers but otherwise remains unaltered and is an unabridged version of the original.

Gleanings from the Records
of Zephaniah Job,
of Polperro

BY

FRANK H. PERRYCOSTE

I suppose that in his time no other inhabitant of Polperro was so widely known as Zephaniah Job, "The Smugglers' Banker": and over a hundred years after his death his name is still familiar. He was, however, not only agent and banker for smugglers and privateers, but also a merchant in a large way of business and, evidently, steward or general man of business to sundry landed proprietors and others in the neighbourhood, for whom he did all sorts of work that would nowadays probably devolve on a family solicitor: moreover, he farmed, drew people's wills, owned barges, and was in short, a man of prodigious and multifarious activity - as the story will show. By the good natured courtesy of the present Messrs. Job, his great great-nephews, I have been able to examine at leisure a collection of account-books and correspondence still preserved at Crumplehorn Mill. There must be over half-a-hundredweight of account books and debris thereof still extant, although their original weight is diminished by the loss of the covers of so many: and there are twenty-five pounds of letter books. What actual tonnage of such material was extant when Job died early in 1821 is a question that "imagination boggles at" and one that will never be answered. It is known that certain malefactors made a huge bonfire of much material: and nobody can guess what documents were then destroyed, though one may doubt whether any ledgers or other such big volumes were consumed in this great bonfire. Long years afterwards the late Mr. Job, great-nephew and namesake of old Zephaniah, gave at least one volume to a niece living in Australia. It seemed to me probable that this was the missing ledger of 1815 to 1820 mentioned below: but I have been assured it was a letter book - in that case probably the last of the series. However, the last ledger is also missing.

While fully appreciating the family feeling that prompted the gift to the Australian cousins - "they had as much right to the books as we had," said one of the present Messrs. Job to me - one must deeply regret that the then custodian of these records did not realise the great importance of retaining intact what was left of this locally valuable collection: for what went to Australia is now almost as effectually lost as what perished in the bonfire. In lamenting such losses, however, I am endorsing the grievance of the historian: but I must confess that, in the end, my own personal feelings verged perilously near unhallowed regret that the salvage had been so great. I understood at first that there were "only" several daybooks and ledgers, two small other volumes, and some big letter-books: and even so there seemed plenty for me to do: but my interest in these records, and my insistence on their value, so aroused Messrs. Job's interest that they disinterred about forty pounds' weight more from a loft in which they had been decaying. I had played the part of Frankenstein only too successfully: and the task of sorting disarticulated fragments and piecing them together into their respective volumes, and cataloguing the whole collection, was imposed by the monstrous pile confronting me as the preliminary to the work of examination and extraction.

Now the object of the catalogue that I have compiled is by no means simply to facilitate references on my own part: for in such case very much of it might have been omitted. This collection of records seems to me of very great value, as a huge quarry for social and economic data of various kinds and of both local and general interest during forty or fifty momentous years — a value that will necessarily increase as, with the progress of time, the past becomes more and more remote: and I cherish the hope that eventually the whole collection may find its way to some West Country museum or library, where it will be carefully preserved and rendered available for consultation by students. In that case the subjoined catalogue will save any such students the loss of I know not how much time and trouble, especially as I have packed up each coverless volume of collected fragments, and some small covered volumes, separately, and have docketed each packet in correspondence with the following catalogue.

* * * * *

Here, however, a very brief digression must be allowed me concerning an item not included in the catalogue. Couch tells us in his history of Polperro that, when Job fled hither from St. Agnes, he endeavoured at first to make a living by keeping a school, but found no great demand for his services as a teacher. There has been preserved with the collection at Crumplehorn an arithmetical exercise-book of one of his scholars. On the first page is the multiplication table, beautifully inscribed, with "John Clements of Polperro" above and "12th December, 1775" below. The book is occupied partly by problems and exercises worked out and partly by tables of weights and measures - decked with many pen and ink flourishes and ornamentations: but many pages were left unused. One page is devoted to directions for applying the 'Golden Rule or Rule of 3 direct': and these directions naturally follow the ancient infamous method of giving a working rule instead of explaining the reason. Teachers in those days, and for long afterwards, had not the slightest notion that the unitary method was here the true golden rule, or that the concrete must precede the abstract in education. Several of the problems and exercises set and worked out are amusing. On the enquiry - "How many Waggans will reach from Fowey to Looe it being Computed 8 Miles; Alowing 6 yards for the Standing of Each Waggan" - my only comments are that Job's computation of distance would be close to accuracy for an aeroplane, but failed for road mileage; that the profusion of capital letters was clearly characteristic of the age; and that the handwriting is so incomparably better than the spelling here and throughout the book that, if it was Clements' own, Job must have been an amazingly good writing master. The enquiry as to the number of seconds in 38 solar years might render one only somewhat restive: but the orders to reduce 7842 miles to barleycorns, and the reverse, and to ascertain how many barleycorns would be required to reach round the globe, seem calculated to reduce one's brain to flitters. Job's passion for myriads of figures was manifest in his teaching as afterwards in his business.

In later years, occasionally from 1787 to 1808,

Clements used some of the blank pages of his school book for accounts with Job for expenses on the Polperro schooner, and for one or two entries which show that he joined the great fraternity of Polperro smugglers — of whom there is much to say in due course.

I think that this precious little relic of ancient schooldays should find a home in some local educational museum.

THE CATALOGUE.

The three volumes 1, 2, and 3, no doubt passed into Job's hands when he became steward or business-manager and banker to Sir Harry Trelawny. (From all those asterisked I have made no extracts whatever: but for special enquiries the information to be obtained from them might be very valuable.)

*1.— Size 12½ inches by 8: no covers: in fragmentary condition, and possibly very incomplete. Accounts of Trelawny estate 1752-1788 - apparently rents of cottagers and others. (This would be very useful to anyone listing the surnames in parishes on the Trelawny estates).

2.— Size 13 by 8: no covers: in bad condition from damp. Accounts January, 1788 to October, 1796 (with 1794 missing) of William Wills as estate steward to Sir Harry Trelawny, debiting Trelawny with the men's wages, and crediting him with sales of corn, milk, butter, animals, wood, etc. - including sales to the "house".

(This is a sheer quarry for prices, as it would be also for wages, if one knew which were names of men receiving full pay, and which those, perhaps, of big boys and youths at a lower rate).

3.- Size 16 by 6¼: no covers: otherwise in good condition. Accounts November, 1787 to

September 1796, of William Wills as house-steward to Sir H. Trelawny. (Every item of housekeeping expenses, and all sorts of other items, paid by him, were scrupulously entered: and one wonders whether it was the fixed rule that all the cash in the house should be in his charge, since there are continually entries of cash - even halfcrowns and shillings – "advanced to Sir Harry". He functioned also as almoner: for there are innumerable entries, often many on one page or several in a day, of "6d. to a poor woman", varied by "1/-to a poor man", and 2/6 to some other, e.g. Wills obtained his supplies of cash chiefly from Job - five or ten guineas at a time, and larger sums other times: but various sales of faggots, and other items, were also brought into account.

4. Size 8 by 6: a thin volume (the parchment cover of which is part of some French legal document or deed of some sort), containing the accounts, 1779 to the end of 1786, of rents, etc. collected for Susanna Eastcott and per con. Job's disbursements for her. This was, no doubt, compiled for her executors.

5. Size 15 by 10: no covers: very tattered fragments of a book of sales of lime from Shallowpool and Polperro and Lerryn, and possibly from kilns elsewhere, and ranging at least from 1788 to 1809.

6. Size 15 by 10: no covers: a thin volume (or its residue) of sales of lime and ashes from 1794 to 1808.

(Probably there has been much loss or destruction of lime records).

7. Size 12½ by 8: no covers: comprising the accounts. 1784-1790 of John Grigg & Co. with various buyers of corn. How much may be missing from the end cannot be known

*8. Size 12¼ by 8½: no covers: accounts 1792-1796 of Job and Grigg with corntraders and others. There is no telling how incomplete this may be.

The next five are of the size 7¾ by 6¼: and should be 1 inch thick when complete. They record purchases of corn at Looe, and sometimes at Polperro, and the sales of clover and trefoil seeds.

9. In 1786 and 1787 (with one page for December. 1784 and about 1½ pages for 1785).

10.— From September 1787 to autumn 1789. (This volume is possibly incomplete).

11.— From December 1791 to summer 1792 : incomplete; and no covers.

12.— From September, 1793, to September, 1795.

13.— 1812 to 1821: no covers: incomplete: (no oats recorded in what remains of this volume).

14.— Size 12 by 8 by 2: no covers. Accounts from November 1788 to early summer 1792, of Job and R. Grigg with countless individuals for timber (and also oars and spars) supplied.

15.— 7¾ by 6¼. Accounts of river-barges 1795—1798. Only very few pages were used; unless, as seems probable, much is missing before 1795 - and then the book was superseded. (After Job's death his nephew Ananiah utilized the book for his own accounts in 1824, etc.)

*16.—Size 12½ by 7¾: no covers: only 34 leaves extant. Accounts 1792-1811 of river barges, a deal in linen (1800-1801), and oddments.11

*17.—Size 15 by 10: no covers: a remnant of over 34 leaves. A mixed lot of accounts, 1786— 1811, of various sorts including arrears for coal, barge accounts, lime-kiln accounts, and with all sorts of people.

*18.—Size 16 by 10: no covers: over 100 leaves of trading accounts, 1793-1810, with various people and including some limekiln accounts, timber (deals) accounts, and the Polperro schooner accounts.

*19.—Size 15 by 10: no covers: in very many pieces and fragments - some partly torn away. Accounts, 1799-1818, with innumerable persons for goods supplied and for "drawings" (i.e., drafting leases) and "writings"; and including "incidents", i e., payments by Job. I cannot guarantee that all the "disjecta membra", which I have now decently re-interred in lot 19, really belong to one and the same very vile "corpus".

20—Size 7¾ by 6¼: thin. Accounts, 1791-1796, with various individuals, largely if not chiefly employees and workmen, and comprising chiefly debts to Job, but occasional credits to one or another.

*21.—A "penny exercise book" but, of course, of the usual handmade paper. Accounts, 1796-1798, with workmen, lime-burners, bargees, a skipper, and others.

*22.—Size 9 by 7½: only a few pages. Accounts 1800-1806 (but with most of the intervening years missing) of William Soady with Job and Rice for timber (deals). Probably Soady was a collector of payments by timber-buyers.

*23.—Size 12 by 7½: only a few pages. Edward Soady's accounts, 1814-1816, with Job for collection of rents and payments.

*24. — Another "penny exercise book". Accounts February. 1810, to March, 1811, of, presumably, the skipper of the Polperro schooner for his payments on pilotage, Customs, harbour dues, food, small repairs, cargoes of coal and culm - totalling £758 in twelve months.

*25.—Size 15½ by 10½ by ½: no covers; remains of a ledger. Accounts with innumerable people, compiled apparently after Job's death to clear up accounts with all indebted to him. There is no telling how much, if any, may be missing from this.

The next seven are all of the size 16 by 6 or 6½.

26. — Daybook, ¾-inch thick, from 16th April. 1782, to 30th April, 1790.

27. — Daybook from April, 1790, to June, 1798.

28. — Daybook, 1½-inches thick from September, 1798, to 20th December, 1808. There are no covers and the book is in over twelve pieces. Parts covering about 21 months are missing; and one cannot say how much additionally may be missing after 1808.

(Obviously a daybook between Nos. 28 and 29 must have disappeared entirely).

29. — Daybook, 1½-inches thick, from 31st December, 1814, to 6th October, 1820 - annotated inside the back cover "This day book posted and examined William Minard".' (This one of many Wm. Minards was clearly Job's clerk.)

The next four I call subsidiary or parallel daybooks. They are crowded with entries, debiting deliveries of lime and corn, with entries of wages to Job's farm labourers, and contain innumerable other entries which also could not be posted into the bank ledger, either because the debtors had no banking account with Job, or because - in some cases - the entries were eventually totalled into one ledger entry. There must have been enough cross-entries and complications almost to glut even Job's insatiable lust for figures. Some of the entries however, especially perhaps when in Job' s own clear vigorous handwriting - for these subsidiary daybooks were mainly kept by a clerk - seem to me to belong rather to the normal series, or anyhow to concern clients with banking accounts: and in one or two instances an entry was deleted and marginally relegated to "the other daybook". With these explanations I continue the catalogue.

30. — No covers, in fourteen pieces, and much

damaged in parts. Daybook from 22nd June 1802, to the end of 1806. Fourteen months in all are missing between these dates. The end of the book is definitely present and so marked.

31.—No covers: in seven or eight pieces partly torn and in poorish condition. Daybook from February, 1807, to end of May 1808. (Obviously a section is missing for the first six weeks of 1807) This daybook is thinner than the others.

32.—Daybook, 1-inch thick, from 28th May, 1808, to 6th July, 1811.

33.—Daybook, from 15th July, 1811, to May, 1814. No covers: very largely destroyed by mice, and their leavings damaged by damp, after January, 1813, and in generally shocking condition.

(I incline to infer that Job abandoned the subsidiary series after this date; and that No 29 functioned as both normal and subsidiary daybook.)

34.—Ledger 16 by 6½ by ¾, from March, 1778, to 1786 (with a few entries of later date).

35.—Ledger, 15 by 10 by 2½, from 1787 to 1800 (with a few entries up to 1805).

36.—A similar ledger, 3 inches thick, from 1801 to 1816, with no covers and in over twenty-four pieces. The first thirty-four leaves and five others are missing: an unknown number - at least fifteen - are missing after folio 357; and over twenty-four leaves are partly destroyed.

(There is positive proof from an account carried forward to "the new ledger" that a final ledger has disappeared).

37.—Cash book, 7½ by 6¼ by 1½, from December, 1808, to May, 1820, but with October and December, 1819, missing. Presumably this records monies paid into and out of Job's bank.

*38.—Size 12¾ by 8: no covers: from 1789 to 1801, but with gaps; and more may be missing before 1789 and after 1801. This book contains full records of drafts by whom, on whom, to whom payable, of whom received, to whom actually paid, with dates and values; and it clearly belongs to the banking series.

*39. — Letterbook. 12 by 8¼ by ¾, from 1st January, 1781, to 26th April, 1785.

*40. — Ditto, 13 by 8¼ by 1¼ from 28th April, 1785, to 15th July, 1789.

*41. — Ditto, 15 by 10 by 1: no covers: from May, 1793, to April, 1795.

(Probably about three-fifths of this volume - namely from July, 1789, to May, 1793 - are missing. This seems to me more probable than that an entire letterbook between 40 and 41 is missing.)

*42. — Ditto 15 by 9½ by 2¼, from April, 1795, to November, 1800.

*43. — Ditto, 15 by 10 by 2: no covers: from January. 1801, to November, 1818.

Even with the covers of two gone, and so much of No. 41 missing, these letterbooks weigh 25½ pounds. They contain, in, all, 1,159 closely covered leaves (i.e., 2,318 pages): and I find that the total area of Job's correspondence thus preserved covers 2.160 square feet, i.e. practically one-twentieth of an acre.

As regards letter-writing Mr. Micawber would seem to have been a puny infant when compared with this epistolary giant. Not only have I not attempted even to skim over any of these volumes, but I have carefully abstained from promising myself to tackle them hereafter. Very probably they contain an immense amount of most interesting information, both about strictly local affairs and about smuggling and privateering, mixed with very much merely formal business correspondence: but it seems quite possible that they might provide any student of those times with many months of hard work. Possibly some such student at some future date may find opportunity and inclination for the work.

Finally, there is a packet of deeds which, at the time of writing this, I have not yet sorted, but which I hope to examine in due course. I can see that many refer to the manor of Rafiel and include several years "Rentals" thereof giving the names of the tenants and the descriptions and rents of their holdings.

*　　*　　*　　*　　*

It must be fairly obvious that, even with all the correspondence put aside, the possible harvest from these records is far too great to be reaped by a series of articles: and I cannot guess what sized volume - or possibly how many volumes! - might be required to deal adequately with all the material possessing interest or value as local or economic or social history. It was imperative to make selections only from the huge mass of material: and, though same other workers might take much that I have left or despise some that I have taken, I hope that, on the whole, what follow are fairly representative gleanings.

JOB'S MERCANTILE ACTIVITIES.
THE SALE OF LIME.

I propose to deal first with Job's various mercantile activities before passing on to the other matters - his stewardships and banking, local history, prices, wages, rents, smuggling, privateering, etc. - on which the daybooks and ledgers yield so much information. From No. 6 we learn that from 1794 to 1808, both included. Job was supplying lime and "ashes" to farmers and others from kilns at Shallow pool (on the West Looe River, about 2½ miles above Looe) and Polperro; that from 1798 he was supplying lime from kilns at Looe also; and that in 1806 and 1807 he was drawing on "Lerryn New Lime Kiln" likewise. One of the later discovered fragments just chanced to mention the old kiln at Lerryn too. When I drafted my first account of this lime-burning business there was no evidence in my hands beyond that afforded by No. 6: but it seemed clear that so large a business could not have sprung suddenly into existence in 1794; and that, as Job sold lime and ashes to the value of probably nearly £3,000 in 1806, he must either have continued the business for many years longer, or have sold the kilns at a satisfactory price after 1808. The records subsequently disinterred and handed over to me proved the correctness of both inferences. From the shocking wreckage of No. 5 one can make out definitely that lime from Shallowpool and Polperro was sold at least "as early" as 1788 and 1792 respectively: and a mighty stream of entries in the daybooks carries the lime-business into 1820. We can date Job's acquisition of the Polperro kilns within fairly narrow limits. In 1789 Thomas Eastcott's account was credited with £8 rent for the limekilns from Richard Barrett: during the next five years the same rent for the kilns was credited to Eastcott without any indication of the tenant: but in 1795 and 1796 the rent was entered definitely from Job and Grigg. I can find no such entry after 1796. Now, since it seems improbable that Barrett would have rented any kilns but those in Polperro; and since the Eastcott family owned various properties in Polperro - as will be shown later; it seems pretty certain that the Polperro kilns were those in question. Since, moreover, Job was supplying lime from them in 1792, it seems clear that he – or he and Grigg acquired the tenancy before 1795 and possibly as early as 1790 - when Barrett was no longer specified as tenant. I surmize that Job may have bought these kilns in 1797: but, if so, either there is no entry in the ledger, or I have overlooked it, in spite of special search. It may be worth adding that these kilns, two in number, stood in Polperro Harbour on ground now occupied by Beach House and/or Messrs. Dunn's pilchard factory, and that the ruins were still there 40 years ago.

Of the history of the Shallowpool kilns I have found nothing: and there is some puzzle about the Looe kilns. In No. 27 there is the following entry dated 27th January, 1796: —

"Paid Mr. John Baker my one half Share of the Purchase Money for the Lime Kilns End Premises at Sandplace Fifty-two Pounds ten shillings": but curiously enough there is no entry of this purchase to Baker's credit in Job's bank-ledger account with him. We seem justified in the inference that Grigg was Job's partner in this purchase: but whether these Sandplace kilns were the same as those elsewhere described as at Looe, and whether Grigg's partnership extended to the kilns at Shallow-pool and Lerryn, and how long the partnership lasted, are questions that I cannot answer. I incline to surmise, however, that the Sandplace kilns were the original Looe kilns: but in January, 1803, Job records "Paid Major Nicholas for the purchase of the Land of a Lime Kiln and Gardens in East Looe and the Lease of Deal yard on New Quay there £177". Whether this kiln replaced or supplemented those at Sandplace we do not know: but on the latter supposition Looe lime had henceforth a double origin.

At some date before 1816 Job acquired an interest in a kiln at Millandreath: but his entry in 1819 regarding "my half concern in Millandreath lime kiln" proves that he was not sole owner. Another entry, of several, told me that for Lerryn kilns Job paid a conventionary rent to the Rashleighs.

It appears from the daybooks that it was customary or very usual to hold a "lime feast" early in the year, at which Job's customers settled their accounts with him: but, since in some cases the heading is definitely "lime paying", one wonders whether this was only a variant for "lime feast", or whether Job sometimes collected his dues without feasting his customers. I have noted "Lime feast at Mr. Perkins's Lerrin" on 30th December, 1806, Lerrin lime feast at Lanreath in January, 1809, at Trecangate in February, 1810, and on 15th January, 1812, lime paying on 11th January, 1813, the feast on 11th January, 1815, the paying at Trecangate on 2nd February, 1816, and the feast at Trecangate on 2nd February, 1817, and somewhere on 8th January, 1818, and the paying on 7th January, 1819.

Similarly there are records of Polperro lime feast on 13th January, 1808, on 10th January, 1812, in February, 1815, on 15th January, 1816, and 13th January, 1818, and of Polperro lime paying on 13th January, 1817, on 13th January 1819, and 3rd January, 1820. I have also noted Shallowpool lime feast in January, 1810, Shallowpool and Looe lime paying on 1st January, 1813, "lime feast at Mr Job's for Shallowpool, Looe and Millendreath, Kilns" on 2nd January, 1816, and a lime feast at Job's for Shallowpool and Looe on 1st January, 1818. There is proof that the kilns at Lerryn and Looe and Millandreath were in commission in 1820. Job died at the end of January, 1822.

I turn now to the mainly fairly-well preserved records in No. 6 from which much of interest can be gleaned. The enormous quantity of lime sold demonstrates the great importance of lime in the agriculture of those days: and to farmers the story should be of special interest. In the following tables I have omitted fractions of bushels, and have given prices to the nearest pound. Actually these prices include not only the lime but also small quantities of "ashes": but the prices of these ashes were only very small percentages of the total prices. For instance, against 7,450 bushels of lime from Polperro kiln in 1796 there were sold 319 – bushels. I suppose – of ashes. The prices then were 18d. per bushel for lime in small quantities, and 14.1d. in large quantities, whilst ashes cost 9d. Thus of the £450 in the table for lime and ashes the latter accounted for barely £12. It may be noted that in 1806 the prices of lime were 16d for quantities but still 18d. for small amounts. I noticed that some ashes were sold at 1s. in 1793.

Since writing the foregoing I have discovered definite proof that Eastcott was still the "owner" of the Polperro kilns in 1810. He held them by a conventionary rent to the manor of Rafiel: and very probably Job bought them in 1811 when the manor was broken up.

QUANTITIES AND VALUES OF LIME SOLD

	At Shallowpool		At Polperro	
in	bushels	£	bushels	£
1794	11,066	620	3,889	220
1795	13,298	777	3,822	227
1796	16,578	988	7,450	450
1797	15,611	912	6,614	388
1798	11,422	671	6,471	380
1799	13,187	842	5,436	350

	At Shallowpool		At Polperro	
1800	14,793	948	6,018	389
1801	not totalled by Job			
1802	not totalled by Job			
1803	not totalled by Job			
1804	13,349	888	7,257	481
1805	17,734	1172	9,542	630
1806	20,280	1336	10,241	674
1807	not totalled by Job			
1808	not totalled by Job			

	At Looe	
in	bushels	£
1798	1,607	95
1799	3,165	199
1800	4,378	275
1801	not totalled	
1802	not totalled	
1803	6,248	427
1804	4,013	259
1805	7,924	453
1806	9,218	567
1807	not totalled	
1808	not totalled	

The Lerryn supplies of 1806-1807 were also left untotalled by Job: and there really seemed no obligation on me to spend considerable time in adding up the individual entries in each such case of default.

The lime-book gives us year by year the names of all the purchasers and the quantities and consequent charges debited to them. I have copied the lists of sales from the Polperro kiln in 1796 and 1806, both as typical samples, and because all sorts of interest attach to the names in such lists.

Sales from Polperro Kiln in 1796

	£	s.	d.
Charles Guy senior	2	1	8
Z. Job	1	15	7
Thomas Rendle	4	14	11
John Bettinson	5	14	11
Wm. Hitchens junior	17	15	9
Thomas Peake senior	3	2	10
Thomas Peake junior	2	8	2
Jos. Menear	1	14	2
Wm. Giddy	12	3	0
James Alger	11	17	4
Richard Lightfoot	10	6	8
John Harris	29	7	0
Isaac Sargent	13	11	6
James Hill	24	19	0
Robert Rean	16	10	0
William Marks	10	5	4
Charles Hutton	4	1	1
George Coath senior	26	5	4
Nicholas May	18	18	1
John Grigg	7	1	0
John Cossentine	7	18	8
Wm. Hitchens senior	12	3	4
John Luke	5	16	4
Charles Turner	5	13	7
Thomas Cook	1	13	6
Wm. Sargent	30	9	4
George Coath junior	15	4	11
Thomas Bartlett	10	6	9
James Pearse	6	11	1
Cornelius Roose	10	8	3
Richard Collings	14	8	2
James Roberts	18	17	3
Jos. Turner senior	2	16	5
Peter Bennett	2	11	6
Margaret Pine	1	15	4
Walter Stephens	3	8	8
Wm. Hocken	21	0	0

James Pearse junior	1	15	4
Charles Guy junior	5	3	10
Thomas Chark	3	10	6
John Pearse	3	19	6
Wm. Powne	8	9	2
John Bate	6	12	3
Wm. Courtice	5	9	11
Edward A'Lee	3	1	3
John Jose	1	11	9
Giles Collings	1	9	11½
Edward Soady	1	19	9
Margaret Hicks		9	0
John Langmaid		4	6
(Ashes only) Wm. Quiller	1	7	9
Philip Littleton		3	0
Ez. Rickard		8	3
Wm. Minards senior		9	0
Richard Mutton		17	3
Wm. Hill		4	6
John Rundle			4½
Wm. Johns junior		9	9
Mary Jasper			4½
Elizabeth Perry			4½
John Rickard		4	6
The Quays	1	3	3
Ann Eastcott	1	0	3
(Ashes only) John Jeffery		12	9
(Ashes only) Reginald Barrett		9	9
Charles Dyer		4	6
John Congdon		9	0
Reginald Barrett junior		1	6
Mr. Eastcott		9	9
Mr. Carpenter		18	0
(Ashes only) Thomas Rendle		3	0
Edward Soady		6	9
Wm. Marks			4½
Wm. Courtis		3	4½
Charles Dyer		2	3

Sales in 1806

	£	s.	d.
James Algar	13	4	8
John Andrew		13	10½
George Aunger			6
John Bettinson	6	16	6
(Ashes only) Wm. Barrett			9
(Ashes only) Wm. Bunt		1	6
George Coath senior	10	18	5
Thomas Charke	18	4	0
George Coath junior	18	7	3
John Cossentine	10	12	7
Hannah Collins	13	2	8
Giles Collins	3	12	10
John Cossentine junior	2	17	3
Richard Couch		16	6
Thomas Ede	24	18	7
T. S. Eastcott	3	15	2
Richard Fiddock	4	2	0
Charles Guy	8	19	5
James Hill junior	35	12	5
John Harris junior	26	15	4
John Harris	40	8	6
Charles Hutton	7	1	1
Peter Hitchens	15	8	3
John Hocken	57	2	10
Arthur Hoskin	11	12	9
Wm. Hocken	18	16	4
Stephen Hoskin	3	5	0
Wm. Hitchens	5	0	9
Wm. Higgens		5	8
Zephaniah Job	84	6	6
Thomas Johns		2	9
Richard Keast	1	11	9
John Leach	33	1	2
Richard Lightfoot	37	13	5
Samuel Langmaid	1	19	0
George Leach		10	6
Philip Littleton		3	0

John Libby	2	3	8
Richard Mutton	3	3	0
Wm. Marks	5	14	9
Joseph Menear		15	0
Wm. Oliver	9	1	5
Thomas Peake	2	13	5
James Pearse	34	15	7
Richard Pollard	11	9	6
(Ashes only) Wm. Powne		18	3
Joseph Pearse		2	3
Thomas Rendle	1	16	9
Cornelius Roose	10	10	9
Thomas Rowe	17	2	7
Richard Rowett (Lively)			6
John Rendle		4	11
Edward Soady			6
Ben Sargent	14	18	4
Samuel Stap	18	19	8
(Ashes only) James Trehane			9
Joseph Turner	2	8	2
John Wyatt	3	9	0
Rebecca Whetter	1	9	11

£674 2 5

The lime amounted to 10,241 bushels 3 pecks, and the ashes to 238 bushels – or whatever the measures for ashes were.

Now it is obvious that the great majority of the names on these lists are those of farmers: and, not only may we reasonably assume that most of these were parishioners of Talland and Lansallos, but actually most of them are already known as such from the Records of these parishes previously published. The Cossentines however have – I believe – farmed in Pelynt for centuries: and, if any Cossentine had farmed in Talland or Lansallos at this period, we should undoubtedly have found his name in the lists of overseers and wardens and employers of parish apprentices. Since it thus appears that at least one family of farmers in Pelynt took lime from the Polperro kiln, there is at least the possibility that several other names in the lists not hitherto found recorded for Talland or Lansallos, may belong to Pelynt: but any such doubtful names are very few indeed. My reason for copying none of the Shallowpool and Looe lists is that, although they no doubt included the names of some Talland farmers in the East of the parish, the great majority must naturally have belonged to Pelynt and Duloe and Morval and St. Martins.

I have noted the following names of customers at the Polperro kiln not occurring in the 1796 or 1806 list.

In		£	s.	d.
1794	Captain Meggs		6	8
	James Puckey	5	12	9
1795	Edward Parsons	4	1	9
	Thomas Shapcott	1	4	0
1801	John Courtis	3	19	0
	Nicholas Snell	1	12	4
1802	An Evea		9	7
	Wm. Roose	1	15	0
1803	John Bellamy		9	9
	Wm. Northcott		7	10
	Wm. Roose		12	0
	John Toms	8	6	4
	Thomas Wakeham	1	6	7
	Thomas Whitter	1	19	6
1804	John Batten	1	16	4
	Thomas Botting		2	2
	John Pascho		6	0
	Robert Hicks		2	3
1805	Michael Hickey		9	0
1807	John Pachyn	1	12	6

For special reasons, to be explained hereafter, I took from the Shallowpool lists the following names:-

In		£	s.	d.
1794	Jane Puckey	4	19	2
	(And she took 105 bushels in 1792)			
	Nathaniel Toms	14	17	0
1795	Nathaniel Toms	19	3	6
	James Puckey	10	6	0

Besides John Morshead in 1794.

Now of the non-farmer minority in then foregoing lists Eastcott and Carpenter were landowners; Soady was a mason, as was also John Congdon; and Littleton and Northcott were, likely enough, the names of masons then as now. The women and others, who bought a few pennyworth of lime, no doubt required it for whitewashing their cottages: while the men, other than masons, who took a few shillingsworth, may have had gardens or allotments. Quiller, although a notable smuggler and privateer, rented some land at one time – of which I shall have to speak later. The name of Captain Meggs is interesting because, while the Bevil monument in Talland church indicates an intermarriage with a Meggs, I had not elsewhere found the name hereabouts. What Job did with the immense amount of lime debited to himself I could not guess until I lit on his farming accounts: and I leave it open whether "Lively" was the name of Rowett's boat or his own nickname. Finally – for future reference – I draw special attention to the entries against John and William Courtis, William Marks, Wm. Roose, Jane and James Puckey, Cornelius Roose, John and Nathaniel Toms, William Oliver, and three of the Collings or Collins family.

"OATES AT LOOE"

When I wrote the first draft of this section, No. 12 was the only book of the corn-trade series in my hands and was naturally supposed by me to be the only survivor: and in that volume "oates at Looe" took so prominent a place that the title for this section seemed ready made, although barley and wheat at Looe were also in evidence and barley and oats at Polperro. Whether the great trade in oats was finally abandoned, or whether at least a third part of No. 13 has disappeared, we do not know: but the latter supposition is far more probable, especially as I found the barley and wheat sections quite separate, and reckoned them at first as (parts of) distinct books. In 12 there is nothing to show whether the grain was bought from or sold to the farmers around: while the fact that a few pages record definitely the sales of clover and trefoil seeds to them might naturally prompt the inference that this was a sales book entirely and that the farmers were buying seed corn! However No. 10 cleared away all ambiguity by the heading on its opening pages of "oates taken in at Looe", shortening later to "oates at Looe" and then reverting to the full heading; and so on. This trade was carried on by Job and Grigg i.e. apparently as partners: but nevertheless and very curiously each individual purchase was entered to Job or Grigg, as the case might be, instead of to the firm: and incidentally all oats and barley taken at Polperro were entered to Job alone. Every page was ruled into two sets of money columns, one headed by Job's name and the other by Grigg's. It looks as though the partnership were like that of two sportsmen – each counting his own bag of game. The partner in the earlier years was J. Grigg, but by December 1791 he was R. Grigg; whilst by 1812 Grigg seems to have disappeared altogether from the business, for there are no Job and Grigg headings in No. 13, which otherwise too is ruled somewhat differently from the earlier volumes, and also has at intervals marginal notes of quantities shipped and for whom.

I take this opportunity of expressing my belief that "John Grigg & Co" were simply Job and Grigg: in which case the inclusion of No. 7 with Job's books is no longer surprising. The ground for my belief is that in turning over the pages of the letterbooks I noticed letters – i.e. copies – signed John Grigg and Co., though in Job's writing and mixed up with his other correspondence. The consecutive dates of 8 and 7 – with allowance for missing pages at the end of 7 – and the supersession of J. by R. Grigg before 1792, tally well with this explanation.

It is obvious that this trade must have gone on steadily from 1784 or earlier to 1820, and that Nos. 9 to 13 are the survivors of a more numerous series.

As I have already mentioned, grain was shipped from Looe: and in the daybooks are many entries of payments to women for carrying corn on to the vessels and also for carrying it to the kilns. A farmer recently explained to me that English wheat does not usually get sufficiently sun-dried to stand storage, and must be artificially dried if it is to be stored. This explanation cleared up my little puzzle about putting corn in the kilns. Incidentally these records of the employment of women for the heavy work of porterage throw a painful light on the manners of the times: and later we shall have to consider women's work in the fields.

I did not undertake the tedious work of adding up the interminable figures to ascertain what quantities of grain were bought in any one year: but, as the number of bushels is totalled in each page, one can see almost at a glance that many thousands of bushels annually were bought. To us now-a-days it seems rather wonderful that a little over a century ago in Talland and Lansallos and all the parishes around so much corn – including wheat – was grown that there was a steady trade in it from Looe.

Here – with a forethought to the section on Prices – I must mention a puzzle which I was quite unable to solve unaided. In the English tables of weights and measures – so fearfully and wonderfully made – we are told that eight bushels equal one quarter: and John Clements' exercise-book can be cited as conclusive evidence that Job recognised this relation of bushels to quarters. Nevertheless the evidence of No. 7 e.g. is conclusive that four bushels were reckoned to the quarter. It is not only that, if the quarter contained eight bushels, Job and Grigg were selling corn at just about half the price they gave for it – and although they may have been most delightfully good-natured and altogether charming men, I am positive that they did not carry good nature to this ruinous extreme – but on one and the same page, one can find prices charged per bushel and per quarter, and the latter at four times the former. I had finally given up the puzzle as hopeless: but Mr. Rilstone tells me that he believes that the Cornish bushel equalled two standard bushels – an explanation which I had already considered but had abandoned after consulting John Clements' tables. If this be the explanation, the fact must be borne in mind when we come to consider prices.

A few words may be added about the trade in clover and trefoil seeds, which naturally were sold in the spring. Here too the prices are entered in columns head Z. Job and J. or R. Grigg respectively. Seeds were brought from London in 1788: and of these some were sold at Liskeard and some at Calstock. As one finds on the same page of clover-seed sales that some were "Looe seeds" and some "brought from Callington", I feel uncertain whether the latter were actually obtained from Callington or were the unsold remainder of seeds sent thither: but the latter explanation seems far more probable in every respect, especially as in 1789 there are entries of seeds sold in Liskeard and of seeds brought from Liskeard. All the seeds sold at Liskeard seem to have been sold on Grigg's account; those "delivered at Polperro" in 1789 were sold on Job's: and those "delivered at Looe", were sold, some on Job's account, some on Grigg's. In 1794 "new" clover seeds from Poole were sold at Looe. "New seeds at Waterses." I give up!

In the long lists of farmers who sold corn to Job and Grigg one finds a crowd of names already familiar in the Records of Talland and Lansallos, and of course many more of whom I have taken no note because one cannot tell from which of the many parishes within touch of Looe they came, or whether a few of them may have been hitherto unrecorded inhabitants of Talland and Lansallos. A few names however I have noted for one reason or another. We find Wm. Lego in 1787 and both Wm. and Richard Lego in 1794: and it may be remembered that a William Lego, baker, was one of the West Looe leaseholders under Talland Parish from 1804. It is interesting to find a Jose was farming somewhere in the neighbourhood. This is a very familiar name in the Lizard: but

I was surprised to find it in these parts. When we come to the names of those bringing barley and oats to Polperro, we can feel sure that they belonged either to one of the two parishes or to one very neighbouring. Among these I find in 1798 "Messrs. Northcotts", John Buckthast, Benjamin Steed, "Mr. Rain" (alias "Mr. Rean" in 1794), and our former friends Cornelius Roose and Wm. Cortice, alias Courtice; and in 1794 John Hodge, Richard Pollard, Wm. Courtice again, Mrs. Pine, and John Cossentine – whose farm in Pelynt must evidently have been so situated that it was easier for him to sell corn and buy lime at Polperro than at Looe. Neither Polperro New Road nor Looe New Road was cut until about 1850. I wonder whether Cossentine drove through Longcombe. James Puckey, John Curtis, Nathaniel Toms, and Wm. Toms, seem to have taken their corn to Looe. Puckey bought 41lbs of new clover seeds in 1794, and Wm. Courtis (for a third variant) 56lbs of the Poole seeds. Once more I draw attention to Courtis and Puckey and Toms, because there will be more to say of them later.

It may be worth notice that corn was brought to Looe from places as distant as Lerryn and St. Neot.

THE TIMBER TRADE

The thickness of the volume No. 14 required – although with debtor and creditor columns on the same page – to record the sales of timber in three or four years, indicates that this was pretty big business. The volume is a mine of information on the price of timber, or anyhow of deal, since the sizes and measurements are given, and should afford much matter of interest to carpenters and builders of today. Moreover, since in very many cases both the addresses and the occupations of the purchasers are given, it is to some extent a trade directory of the neighbourhood – for Job and Grigg supplied Duloe, Morval, Pelynt, Lanreath and Liskeard, as well as Looe and Polperro.

The questions now arise – how long did this business continue: and has a long series of timber accounts suffered destruction; or, if the sales continued, were the accounts entered only in No. 18? This volume runs from 1793 to 1810: but I did not search it to find the latest timber entry. No. 22, however, proves definitely the persistence of the trade up to 1806, and also shows that from 1800 to 1806, it was carried on in partnership with Rice. We do not know when this partnership began or ended, or when Grigg dropped out. Odd entries in the day books yield the following information. Job was apparently still selling timber in 1810, whilst in 1816 he seems either still to have sold it on his own account or to have acted as agent for a timber merchant – and the latter seemed to me the more likely interpretation of the entries. This brings us up to within a few years of the close of his life: but I incline to think that timber became, or perhaps had always been, of far less importance than corn and lime.

I should add that in many cases the entries in No. 14 of payments are followed by Job's or Grigg's signatures, and that many of the latter are those of R. Grigg thus already acting for J. Grigg.

BARGES AND VESSELS

Water transport is perhaps the next business of this very busy man to be considered. We learn from No. 15 that at least as early as in 1795 he was financially interested in barges plying on the Looe River. How much earlier he may have been interested in these barges cannot be determined: for I noticed no barge accounts of earlier date in the relics of Nos. 16 and 17. I have said advisedly that he was financially interested in the barges in 1795: for it seems clear that he was only part owner or partner in the profits. I strongly suspect that in the course of time he either bought out or otherwise disposed of his partner or partners in the barges – and likely enough of those in lime and timber, as evidently in corn – and acquired in each case the entire business: but it would require an exhaustive and intolerably exhausting examination of thousands of pages of accounts to determine this question – and the possibly decisive pages might be among those lost! It seems probable enough, however, that in early days his partners found the essential capital, while Job furnished the brain-power and limitless energy; and that later he was able to finance all these businesses himself.

I think that the river barges were very largely utilised for bringing culm to the limekilns at Shallowpool and Sandplace; and bargeloads of culm were brought to Polperro – in calm weather, presumably: but I find also cargoes of bricks, coals, deals and sand , for instance. There are accounts of 1795, 1796 and 1797 with Charles Bowden for these barges, of 1797 with Edward Parne as master, and of 1798 with Philip Croft as master. I rather think that Bowden was master bargee too or part owner or both.

Various entries enable us to trace the barge business to the end of Job's life. In No. 16 there is a series of barge accounts from 1801 to 1811; but I could not decide how many barges were listed:

and I noted down references to barges in every year, except 1815, from 1814 to 1820 inclusive. In December 1803 he paid £30 5s "on account of a river barge built for me at Looe": and here the "for me" is significant as indicating sole ownership of at least one barge: but during this year he seems to have held one fifth share in the barge 'Endeavour'. In 1809 he paid £150 for a new barge: and I suppose that it was on his own account that he paid £84 6s 6d for building a new barge, the 'Dove', at Fowey. In January 1819 he sold his 3/8 share of the 'William' – but I suspect that this was not a barge but a sea-going vessel. Land and river and sea all brought grist to Job's omnivorous mill: and, if aeroplanes had been invented in his time, he would probably have been financially and administratively interested in several of them. We hear of the schooner 'Polperro' at least as early as 1805 – and I nowise guarantee that this is the earliest reference. In No. 31 are entries of 1807 about the "new schooner", followed soon afterwards by many entries about the schooner 'Polperro': so it seems possible that there were successive schooners of that name. At this time our friend John Clements was skipper: and he is much in evidence in No. 31. In January, 1808, Job "advanced" him £70 8s on account of the schooner: and in February he sent £60 to "Captain John Clements" at Padstow. An entry of 1810 seems also to justify the conclusion that Job was the owner. I have noted a reference to this schooner in 1815: but again I am nowise to be understood as implying that no later entries can be found.

There are entries indicating his part ownership of, or shares in, other vessels: but a Hercules would be required to sort out all the wheat from the chaff of these Aegean stores of records – and a primeval Job to publish the inventory. Something more may be said, however, in this connection when we come to smuggling and privateering.

OTHER MERCANTILE INTERESTS

This section I can dispose of very briefly. A deal in linen is included in No. 16: and there is another reference to this in No. 35, from which I have already learned that at the end of 1800 "M. Dawson Downing Esq., of Rowsgift, Ireland" consigned Irish linens to Bristol and Plymouth and Looe. I rather think that Job acted simply as agent in selling the linen: and one entry in No. 35 suggests that Downing may have been related to, or a friend of, Job's clients the Carpenters – of whom anon.

* * * * *

It seems clear that over a long series of years Job provided Polperro with coal, for which of course he had all the facilities of marine transport. If I interpret correctly a certain entry in a day book, on one occasion he sold at 14s per quarter coal which had cost him 13s 3d. If this was a typical case, he certainly did no profiteering in coal but was an useful public servant at a very moderate remuneration.

I incline to think that on occasions too, he sold bricks - probably, however, only bringing in a small consignment now and then when they were needed.

* * * * *

From No. 35 we learn that he also did something in the way of exporting pilchards. In 1796 he debited B. Nicholas & Co, of Naples, with the value of ½ N.P. of 652 hogsheads of pilchards; and Stickling &

Co., of Leghorn, with "my $1/3$ in 450 hogsheads"; and Porter & Huddart of Leghorn with "my $1/2$ N.P. of 650 hogsheads". These entries are very characteristic of Job and his contemporaries – hereabouts at any rate – as regards the splitting of ventures into shares. One recalls the 400 years earlier precedent of Dick Whittington. "N.P." I cannot interpret. Job's charge to Stickling for his third was $1747/13^{1/3}$ in Italian coinage of that date unknown to me, which at the exchange of 55, represented – quite unintelligibly - £400 9s 7d; and for his half of the 650 hogsheads $3369/5/2$ Italian, which would represent £770. It is interesting to find English firms established in Italy and importing pilchards. In later days the Italians reversed the process by establishing fish "factories" in Polperro and buying direct from the fishermen.

I doubt whether Job did very much in this line of business: but I scarcely think that this series of transactions was unique.

* * * * *

One might suppose that the conduct of all this very varied business, plus the tremendous amount of work as steward to sundry important people and as banker alike to these and to smugglers and privateersmen, would have provided ample occupation for two or three normal men: but, in addition to monopolising all this work, this insatiable worker farmed Killiow during at least the last twenty years of his life. Debits and credits to Killiow Farm are littered through a series of daybooks: and there can be no reasonable doubt that all these were duly posted into a farm ledger – though any such ledger is among the lost volumes. If all farmers kept their accounts as rigorously as Job kept those of Killiow, I suspect that the Oxford School of Rural Studies and the Agricultural Colleges would have little, if anything, to teach them of accountancy. That lost Killiow ledger would nowadays be a wonderfully interesting and valuable find.

At Job's death his farm stock and implements were valued at £398.

* * * * *

As I have already noted, Job also made people's wills: and there seems much reason for inferring that he was generally available as executor or co-executor for his neighbours. Some of the accounts in No. 19 seem to indicate that he also trained himself to draft leases and other more or less legal "writings". It might be objected that his charges for "drawings" were only the fees that he had already paid to lawyers on the lessees' account: but the impression left on me was that he had drafted the leases, etc., himself. It seems to me nowise incredible that this remarkable man – having, of course, plenty of lawyer-drawn leases for examples – should have trained himself sufficiently to the technique required: and to one with his inordinate love of consuming ink and paper the inditing of all the semi-interminable legal rigmarole must have afforded sheer joy. What the local lawyers thought of such poaching on their manors is another question.

This phase of Job's work aptly introduces us to the next section.

———

JOB AS STEWARD

In handing over an early instalment of the
records to me, one of the present Messrs. Job
remarked that Zephaniah had been steward to
Sir Harry Trelawny.

This description of him as steward seemed so
appropriate, when I studied his accounts with
Trelawny and realised what functions he had
discharged, that I decided to classify my notes
on this department of his work for Trelawny and
others under the heading of stewardship – even
if it should not be the fact that he was actually
appointed steward by name. However, as I
found that he collected the manorial rents at the
court leet, I think that he must have been steward
in the technical legal sense to Trelawny and to
others also.

Of all Job's stewardships that under Trelawny
was by far the most important: and I imagine
that it must have been a very proud day for the
quondam refugee from St. Agnes – originally
an aspirant for the post of "captain" of a mine
at home – when in May 1786 he found himself
steward and banker to the greatest landowner
in this neighbourhood, i.e. to "the Rev. Sir Harry
Trelawny, Bart." as Job punctiliously entered
him not only at the head of each ledger-page but
above the countless debits and credits, however
trifling, in his day-books and elsewhere. I have
wondered how many hours – or days? – of his
busy life Job might have saved for his varied
work if he had shortened the entries down to
"Sir H. Trelawny." For this stewardship he
received a salary of £50 per year: and I soon came
to the conclusion that he earned every penny of
his pay – although I have not yet touched his

correspondence with Trelawny, and am prepared to find that prodigious. Not only did he discharge his duties of manorial steward by collecting rents at the annual court leet – presumably holding the court – but he also took over very much of the work of a household steward as described in the catalogue under No. 3. He paid the wages of the domestic and other servants, the rates and taxes – including such personal taxes as hair-powder licences – the school-bills, all sorts of tradesmen's and workmen's bills down to the most trifling items, and apparently nearly everything that fell in the way of a house-steward's disbursements except the sixpences and shillings to poor men and women, and the payments for eggs and fish and poultry, etc., that were taken to Trelawny by the vendors. I was rather puzzled by the fact that Wills' accounts in No. 3 run from November, 1787 to October, 1796, and that he and Job were therefore functioning contemporaneously for at least ten years; whereas, when I discovered Wills' accounts, I had at once inferred, before comparing dates, that he ended when Job began. I surmize that Wills paid what had to be paid at Trelawne on the spot, and that he was probably financially Job's subordinate and rendered accounts to him – in which case one can understand why his books came into Job's possession. It was certainly not the case the Wills paid all the small accounts and Job only the larger: for almost as soon as he took up his appointment one finds Job paying trifling sums of about nine and sixteen shillings for instance; while Wills' fox entries are matched by the following of May, 1797 – "Gave a man a fox, by Sir Harry's orders, 2/6." Job's payments for his employer ranged from large sums down to two or three shillings for fish or 3s 6d for 9½ pints of brandy sent "by the shepherd". He regularly supplied the travel-money when the boys returned to school in London, and even a £1 tip sent by their father's order to one of them. Apparently on all occasions Sir Harry sent to him for whatever cash he required whether at Trelawne or elsewhere in Cornwall: and Lady Trelawny was similarly supplied periodically with money for housekeeping – though one rather wonders what use she can have found for it when Job's payments were so many and so varied. However it is difficult to describe in detail Job's payments as steward without including his role as banker: but I am endeavouring to divide the material, and to deal with Job as banker in a separate section.

Next let us take Job's stewardship to the Eastcott family. Richard Eastcott had been rector of Lansallos from 1789: and it is reasonably certain that Job had been steward or agent for him. I found one loose sheet of paper, dated 1782, giving Job's accounts with Eastcott's executors: and in No. 26 we find plenty of entries to the account of the widow Mrs Susanna Eastcott, then resident in Lostwithiel: but I have no note of any salary paid to him by her. When Mrs Eastcott died at the end of 1786 Job, of course, paid all the funeral expenses; and he thenceforward had an account for some years with her executors, paid school-bills and clothes-bills for her children, and continued to collect their rents and manage their house-property. He drew a salary of five guineas a year for his work and when the son, Thomas Sandford Eastcott, had come of age, and the executors' debit was carried to his account, Job continued to draw the same salary for a time: but after 1794 his salary was raised to 30 guineas. The amount of this salary has always surprised me, since the accounts do not suggest that there was enough work to necessitate such a salary: but, as Job seems to have undercharged rather than overcharged his clients, we may feel assured that he earned this salary too. Eastcott's two sisters paid Job two and half guineas each at first, but later only a guinea each: and after 1800 – or at any rate early in the new century – he seems to have charged no salary against their very small incomes.

The remainder of Job's stewardships can be briefly described. The Carpenter family, who owned the manors of Lansallos and Raphiel, paid him a salary of six guineas: and I incline to wonder whether twice as much would not have been very inadequate – for I have read and copied the rental of one of these manors. Richard Carpenter "of Ireland" paid him one guinea yearly. Benjamin Shipman, rector of Lansallos from 1779(?) to early 1790, and his similarly unworthy successor Henry Pooley, normally paid him three guineas: but in the transition year he got three and a half from Pooley, whilst in 1794 he seems to have drawn only one guinea – I do not understand why. In addition there were extra expenses in connection with the collection of tithes: but usually these were specifically payments to someone other than Job, though in some cases they were possibly or apparently extra payments to himself.

Very early in the nineteenth century Job became steward to Sir Harry's son William Lewis Trelawny, from whom he received a salary of twenty guineas and for whom he paid all sorts of accounts and items, great and small, just as for his father. In Job's daybook and ledger we first meet this son as a schoolboy at Westminster, then find payments for him at Oxford, and later – after the hiatus in No. 36 – find him obviously married and established apparently somewhere in the neighbourhood. He figures under several aliases. In November 1802 Job debits him as Wm. Lewis Salusbury, Esq., with £115 as the balance of the account to Edmund Lange, Esq., "for changing your name": and the extravagantly high fee indicates a royal licence obtained through the College of Arms, since change of name by deedpoll costs only a trifle. By 1800 he had been Captain Salusbury: but it was only after some time, and by tracing accounts through the ledger in order to find out something about this Captain Salusbury who had suddenly appeared and then seemed to disappear, that I discovered his identity with W. L. Salusbury. During the latter part or at the end of 1807 he became W. L. Salusbury Trelawny: and, so far as Job's ledger carries us, that was his final name. I presume that he was the direct ancestor of the late Sir Wm. Salusbury Trelawny.

This section may suitably close with an entry of January 1802 against Job's client Dawson Downing, whom he debits re a legal action "to my writing an indefinite number of letters therein, and several journeys, and expenses, I charge only £2 2s 0d." This is not an unique example, I think, of Job's undercharging. Downing was the consignor of the Irish linens mentioned in an earlier section: and his executors are in evidence in January, 1808.

———

JOB AS BANKER

First of all in this section let us consider Job's banking relations with several of those clients to whom he was also steward. The relation was remarkable: for to these people he was banker not only in the ordinary sense but also and very notably in the schoolboys' slang sense. In other words, instead of making his fair banking profit out of the minimum balance left in his hands he provided over a long series of years the funds on which these clients drew. True he charged them interest on their overdrafts: but during just the same series of years this interest accrued to him on paper only and thus merely swelled the debt to him. Sir Harry Trelawny was the mighty protagonist in this curious game of beggaring the banker: and the story of his dealings with Job is remarkable. The account was opened in May 1786: and in October Job balanced it, sent a copy to Sir Harry, and at once opened a fresh account. (Incidentally he charged no salary at the end of 1786.) The year closed with £243 to Sir Harry's credit: but at the end of 1787 he was already £1,081 in debt. Job was evidently somewhat perturbed: for he recorded in his ledgers in January 1788 – when the account was actually balanced – "and a copy, signed by me, delivered to Sir Harry Trelawny, who returned a copy thereof signed by himself the 4th February, 1788." At the end of 1788 the debt had risen to £1510: whereupon, on 5th January, 1789, "Sir Harry gave me his note of hand for part of the above balance £1,000." Having obtained this note of hand Job felt no further worry or anxiety – so far as one can judge from his ledgers – but allowed Trelawny's debit balance to increase to ten times five hundred pounds, and troubled about no additional notes of hand. This little transformation of a part of the ledger debit into a note of hand – which remained as an extra debt for very many years – puzzled me for some time: but I think that I can explain why the transformation gave Job a very satisfactory sense of security. It was not in the least, I think, that a business debt was converted into a "debt of honour": but under the old laws of debt a creditor could at any instant secure the arrest and consignment to a debtor's prison of anyone whose note of hand he held: whereas I suspect that process against a client, who had overdrawn his banking account, was far less summary and very possibly did not fall under the debt laws at all. If I am in error any legal reader can at once correct me: but I feel pretty sure that my explanation of the security afforded by a note of hand is correct. We seem entitled to assume that Job, as a good man of business, felt quite satisfied that there was security for the ultimate liquidation of the steadily increasing debt to him: and we may also feel assured, I think, that very great mutual respect and esteem developed between the baronet and this invaluable steward and banker during their intercourse of over thirty-four years: but we can also realise that Job's sense of safety during the long years of waiting was appreciably increased by his possession of that note of hand which he retained until the total debt was at last liquidated. The records of the next eighteen years may now be briefly tabulated: and in all statements of money, both in this section and elsewhere, I shall usually ignore shillings and pence. Trelawny's debt to Job at the end of each year was as follows:-

Year	Amount	Year	Amount
1789	....£413	1798	....£4,049
1790	....£1,056	1779	....£5,433
1791	....£1,877	1800	....£3,817
1792	....£2,762	1801	....£3,633
1793	....£3,800	1802	....£3,854
1794	....£3,940	1803	....£4,472
1795	....£4,015	1804	....£4,148
1796	....£4.011	1805	....£2,979
1797	....£3,791	1806	....£2,071

In addition there was still the note of hand for £1,000: so at the peak in December, 1799, he owed £6,400. During twenty years Job's salary and the interest on the debt had been paid to him only on paper, i.e. as additional debit entries against Sir

Harry that merely increased the debt: so that for these twenty years Job had been living – as far as this important client and employer was concerned – simply on great expectations. It is wonderful that he who had arrived here as a youngster compelled to fly from home and probably with not very many shillings in his pocket, and had tried to earn a living by opening a village school, soon raised himself by sheer ability and industry and business capacity to such a position that in middle life he was able to finance his great landed neighbour to the tune of thousands of pounds for twenty years. The final liquidation was sudden. Early in 1807 Sir Harry completed the sale to his son W. L. S. T. aforesaid of Bochym – situated between Helston and the Lizard – for £9,000. With the proceeds he paid off a mortgage on Bochym of £3,000, with which one had made acquaintance in the early days of Jobs accounts, repaid Job the ledger debit and the note of hand, and also repaid sundry smaller borrowings from others. Having cleared off all these liabilities he was left with a credit balance of £858 at the end of March, and £1,114 at the end of the year. During the next eight years (with a record of 1811 missing) his year end balance averaged £1,234, with a maximum of £2,167 at the end of 1808 and a minimum of £358 for 1813. At the end of 1816 he owed Job the trifling amount of £165: and unluckily thenceforth the ledger is missing.

Now the liquidation in 1807 of debts accruing through twenty years was eminently satisfactory to Trelawny and also to Job – on paper: but actually Job remained for a while little better off. The fact is that, while Peter paid Job, he did so by selling to Paul who borrowed from Job in order to pay Peter. In other words the purchase by W. L. S. T. of Bochym was followed by a considerable augmentation of his existing debt to Job: but this introduces the story of Job's dealing with the second generation of this ancient family.

When Wm. Lewis was quite a young man and still at Oxford Sir Harry directed Job to write off from his account all that had been spent on his son since he left Westminster School, and to debit this to an account with the youngster himself. Job, therefore, cancelled these debits to Sir Harry's account, or credited them back to him – although I did not feel certain that some earlier items had thus been credited back; for it seemed to me that there had been some little confusion about the earlier corrections. Anyhow, during two years at Oriel College in 1799 and 1800 the debit against the younger Trelawny ran up to £956 at which stage the amount was carried forward to one of the early missing pages of No. 36. We, therefore, know nothing about the balance in 1801: and the record of 1811 is also missing: but at thirteen year ends the debit to Job was as follows:-

1802 ....£1,844	1809 .... £511
1803 ....£1,659	1810 ....£2,366
1804 ....£2,081	1812 ....£4,032
1805 ....£2,229	1813 ....£3,489
1806 ....£2,166	1814 ....£3,531
1807 ....£2,785	1815 ....£1,671
1808 ....£3,921	

Since the last part of ledger No. 36 and all the following ledger are missing we remain ignorant whether this debt was liquidated in 1816 or later.

Another of Sir Harry's four sons, namely Hamelin, opened an account with Job in 1806, and owed him £457 at the end of the year: but I have no other note of this account than that in August, 1816, he owed Job £292 14s. I formed the impression that Hamelin came into some thousands of pounds on or after marrying: and he had financial transactions with his brother aforesaid in Flintshire.

An account with Sir Harry's elder daughter was opened in 1803: but there were only three or four very trifling credit entries – the last in 1805 – altogether: and then there is an entry at the end of 1815 that the balance due to Job is £2,490 and that on folio 372 interest is charged up to 29th July, 1817. Since, however, folio 372 was in the missing last part of this ledger we cannot know whether this debt was liquidated by Sir Harry or by whom or when.

A very trifling account with the younger daughter, Mary, was opened in 1804: but of this there seems nothing to say.

It appears from the foregoing figures that at the end of 1816 the Trelawny family must have owed Job above £4,000 or more: and it would have been interesting to discover the final liquidation of the conjoined liabilities – had there been no destruction of ledgers. Not only may we assume as before that Job knew perfectly well what he was doing, and that once more his security for the ultimate repayment of all due to him was complete: but we may gauge his affectionate regard for Sir Harry from the tradition in the Job family that he had intended to make him his heir. However, I must not further anticipate the conclusion of my story.

The Eastcott family were clients of the Trelawny type, but on no such magnificent scale. When Mrs. Eastcott died at the end of 1786 or very beginning of 1787 her account was £164 in debt to Job: and the indebtedness of her executors at the next seven year-ends was as follows:-

1787 nearly £50	1791 .... £180
1788 .... £125	1792 .... £195
1789 .... £154	1793 .... £224
1790 .... £201	

The final debt was carried forward to the account of her son Thomas Sandford Eastcott, who was a schoolboy when she died, who blossomed into "Captain Eastcott" in 1797, and is mentioned in 1807 as of the Royal Cornwall Militia. For six of seven years he remained in debt to Job, his year-end debts being:-

1794 .... £405	1797 .... £471
1795 .... £197	1798 .... £671
1796 ....£1,309	1799 .... £699

but at the end of the century only £11 12s 10d. His accounts for 1801, 1810 and 1811 have gone with the lost ledger pages: but for the twelve year-ends extant from 1802 to 1816 his credit balance averaged £651, with a minimum of £265 in 1802 and a maximum of £1,182 in 1812. Thus Job's 14 years' credit to the executors and Eastcott himself was fully justified by the sequel.

The accounts with Eastcott's two sisters were small: but up to the close of our record Job was still a loser by them. At four of the first nine year-ends after her mother's death Miss Eastcott had small balances to her credit: and at the other five she owed Job small amounts. Of 1796 to 1802, both included, I have no information: but the fourteen years 1803-1816 all closed with debits against her, averaging practically £120, and ranging from £96 to a maximum of £226 at the end of 1816. She died in 1817. Her executors owed £217 at the end of the year, and £225 at the end of 1818: and once more the rest is silence. The second sister, Ann, had trifling balances at the first three year-ends, but was in debt to Job at the next six for over £24 on the average: whilst each of the sixteen years 1803 to 1818 ended with an average debt of over £75; and the average of the last seven was £128. Here again, of course, we know not how or when the debt was cleared off. It is a striking fact – unhappily characteristic of this country, at any rate in those days – that, while the brother had a large income, these two unfortunate sisters had only rentals of between £50 and £60 yearly each – unless there was other income which did not pass through Job's hands – and very much out of these trifling incomes went on repairs and conventionary rents.

Fortunately for Job not all his clients required him to finance them for a dozen or twenty years before they kept a credit balance with him: but consequently of these other clients almost nothing need be said. Naturally he was banker as well as steward to the Carpenters: and they figure fairly prominently in his books. They appear first as Sir Jonathan Phillipps Carpenter and J. P. Carpenter (jointly), then after 1798 as Mrs and J. P. Carpenter, and in 1800 as Christian (i.e. Mrs?) and J. P. Carpenter. Before the end of 1802 we hear of Mrs Carpenter's executors; while both in 1806 and 1810, e.g. the account is with J. P. Carpenter and "the Representatives of Thomas Phillipps". I defer further mention of this family to a later section. Robert Grigg, of Looe, was another local client: and his account ran to over £2,900 in 1791-2, nearly £2,800 in 1793, and over £2,500 in 1794. As a contrast there is a small account of only £13 9s from October 1778 to July 1780 with "Mr. James Walter (late) innkeeper in Polperro". Apparently he had the New Inn, of which we hear so much.

In No. 36 I noticed various fresh clients, whom I had not found in the eighteenth century, and among them Lord Grantley. I know nothing of his place of residence: but another client was "of Salisbury".

Patient – or – impatient – readers may object that Job was notoriously "the Smugglers' Banker", and that Trelawny and Eastcott and the rest of these people had nothing to do with smuggling: but, as I said at the opening, Job was not only the smugglers' banker, but very much else besides; and nearly all that has to be said of him in his popularly known role is reserved for the section on smuggling. Our next concern is to consider how interest was charged in Job's day: and the method was very curious and in a sense arbitrary. On 31st December each year Job struck the balance, and found Sir Harry, e.g., indebted to him for so many hundreds or thousands; and on 31st December a year later he charged him interest on this debt, irrespectively of whether the amount had meanwhile been largely increased or reduced. This, when the debt was increased during the current year Job got no interest on such increment – i.e., none during that year, even if there was a large increase in January or February: and when it was decreased by however much and however early in the year, his client nevertheless paid a full year's interest at the year-end on the debt as at the previous 31st December. One may say that on the average the arrangement was as broad as it was long: but by comparison with the modern banking method of striking a balance quarterly and charging interest on so many days overdraft or debt, and repeating the process quarterly, it is clear that Job lost heavily, and in this respect too functioned as banker in the slang sense.

There seems also to have been a curious practice – outside banking – of allowing interest to remain unpaid for many years, and then accepting a lump payment in clearance: and in the records that I have noted it cannot be determined from the figures whether the interest was compound, or whether the lender simply went without his interest for years, and thus obliged his debtor gratis. Here are the data. In 1785 John Quiller lent Sir Harry Trelawny £100: and late in 1799 a lump sum of £76 5s was paid for interest up to August, 1800. Similarly on £100 lent to Job in 1788 he paid £61 13s 4d late in 1799 for interest up to August, 1800: while Grigg, on repaying a loan, paid therewith 3¾ years' interest in a lump sum. Now, if the interest was at 5 per cent, it is clear that neither Trelawny nor Job paid compound interest: and there the matter ends. The difficulty in the way of accepting this solution is simply that Job charged Trelawny only 4½ per cent interest on ledger-debt and note of hand alike until the end of 1797, though 5 per cent, thenceforth: and one would therefore suppose that only 4½ per cent was charged on the loans in question. Compound interest at 4½ per cent would, however, have mounted to sums exceeding those paid: but, according to my calculation, compound interest at 4 per cent would meet the case. Thus I must leave it an open question whether the payments represented simple interest at 5 or compound interest at 4 per cent – with the proviso that, when I extracted the records, I was certainly under the impression that only simple interest was paid, while the question of compound interest arose on later reflection.

During the nineteenth century Job seems to have modified his methods into conformity with modern procedure: for at least as early as 1809 he was charging Hamelin Trelawny interest quarterly. Moreover in 1809 he charged W.L.S.T. interest by days on overdraft, but allowed him interest per con – not, apparently, on his nett balance, but on each individual item credited. I found a loose page of the most appalling calculations, every item debited or credited carrying interest to Job or his client from the date of entry to the end of the year, as it seemed to me! I inferred from the handwriting that Job had deputed his hapless clerk to make – or only to copy? – these heartbreaking calculations: but, if W.L.S.T. checked them, the clerk got the stricken duellist's revenge. I am told that some such system of reckoning interest each way is in vogue today for banking accounts of firms whose credits and drawings run into enormous sums: but I should suppose that interest is charged or given on the nett balance from day to day. I do not guarantee, however, that I mastered the intricacies of the page of calculations: and therefore I will not positively affirm that Job did not reckon interest on nett daily balance.

Two other features of Job's banking remain to be recorded. Firstly, in very early days he charged the various smuggling firms in Guernsey only ½ of 1 per cent on the money paid in to their credit by the Polperro smugglers: but as early as 1782 he raised his charge to 1 per cent. Even so, when he had to remit £1,000, he kept only £10 as commission for his trouble. Secondly, at the end of every year, he regularly debited a client's ledger-account with postage: and this was not merely a temporary practice in early days; for I have a definite note of finding it still in vogue in 1814.

* * * * *

Both in order to meet the requirements of the Guernsey smuggling firms as to the remittance of much of the money due to them, and also to provide credits in London for private and business clients, Job ran into large accounts with various London bankers: but the relative magnitude of the financial transactions carried on by this representative of an insignificant Cornish fishing village – as present-day Londoners would probably describe it – can be realised only by a survey of some of the actual figures. Certainly Polperro must have been very well known in London financial circles in those days.

First of all, let us look at Job's accounts in several early years with William de Jersey, who was evidently banker and agent for privateersmen, arranged for the legal condemnation of their prizes, paid the fees of the proctors and others, and did various financial work. I did not positively satisfy myself whether he functioned also for the Guernsey smuggling firms: but his name is pretty conclusive evidence that he came of their stock; for apparently everyone named "Jersey" had something to do with smuggling in those days!

Job's account with de Jersey from January, 1781, to late September, 1783, ran to £7,390 – leaving a balance of £477 due to Job – besides an account in 1782 of over £141, and one late in 1783 of £1,372, with "Job Quiller and Johns". From December, 1783, to the end of October, 1784, the account, opening with a balance of £477 aforesaid, ran to £728 and closed with a balance of £569 due to Job. I chanced upon a letter in which Job strongly protested against the tremendous and unexpected bill of costs which de Jersey had charged against his privateering clients. He was, perhaps, more of an agent than a banker: but the firms now to be mentioned were clearly bankers, though Perchard & Co. may have been financial agents as well – if one can make the distinction.

From October, 1795, to April, 1796, Job's account with Commerell Lubbock & Co. ran to £2,711. His accounts with Perchard Brock and Lemesurier in the eighteenth century were as follows. In April, 1787, he carried forward from No. 34 to the new ledger £84 to their credit: and at the end of 1788 the total was £705. During the next eleven years there was a notable rise and fall, as exhibited in the subjoined tabulation of these years' accounts

1789 .... £526	1795 ....£3,800
1790 ....£1,052	1796 (to Oct.) £4,391
1791 ....£1,160	Nov. 1796 to Dec.
1792 ....£2,050	1797 ....£1,033
1793 ....£2,600	Mar. 1798 to Oct.
1794 ....£1,500	1799 .... £284

Job's transactions with this firm were not confined to smugglers' business, but included credits for Sir Harry Trelawny: and marine insurance was effected by or through the firm. Some of the Trelawny business reminded me of Mr. Midshipman Easy's pretty way of drawing bills on his father, when he needed funds to meet his expenses afloat and ashore: for just similarly Sir Harry's sailor son drew bills which figure in these accounts alongside of various credits required by Sir Harry himself either for foreign travel or other purposes.

In the nineteenth century I have found the following accounts with Brock and Lemesurier-
1804 - £4,840, leaving over £819 due to B.L.
1805 - £3,979, leaving over £463 due to B.L.
1806 - £3,573, leaving over £1,073 due to B.L.
1807 - £7,343, leaving over £464 due to Job.
1808 - £6,350, leaving over £1,124 due to B.L.
1810 – over £14,500, of which, however, £6,021 had been brought forward from 1809 – the records of which are missing – as balance due to Job.

Finally, as mere samples of Job's dealings with another London bank, his accounts in 1813 and 1814, e.g. with Christopher Smith, Son & Co. – presumably Smith's Bank of later days – ran into many thousands in a year. Incidentally – as will appear later – smuggling can have contributed nothing at this date to Job's banking business which had now become wholly and highly respectable.

I have omitted to say that, unlike, modern bankers, Job entered halfpence and farthings in his ledgers.

AN OLLA PODRIDA OF LOCAL HISTORY

In this section I propose to collect a whole series of trifling records about Polperro between 1780 and 1820. Unhappily – in one sense – they are of so varied and disjointed a character that the problem of arranging them in any satisfactory logical order is scarcely soluble: and I am afraid that to a considerable extent this section will be, not an orderly building, but a pile of bricks and timber, or – to vary the metaphor – not a well defined course, but a veritable olla podrida as I have entitled it. I have tried to effect some sort of arrangement by classifying a few of the records as illustrations of manners and customs, and by putting together, of course, and in chronological order, all records relating to one and the same subject; and I have tried to arrange such groups as exist in some sort of rational sequence: but there remains a residue which forms a mere chronological higgledy-piggledy.

We learn from No. 3 that at Trelawne the "Christmas Players" were given 15s in 1788 and 10s 6d in 1791: but we do not know whether these players were early carollists or late mummers. At Trelawne also, in 1789, a man was given 1s for killing a fox, and another man 2s: and in 1792 half a crown was paid for killing two foxes. Thus Sir Harry was very far less lavish than Talland Parish in paying for "vermin".

In 1788 there are two entries of a guinea on each occasion to men for liquor on launching a new boat. Polperro was not characterised by teetolalism in those days.

There are many entries in Job's accounts of the purchase of lottery tickets for clients: but I have extracted only two as examples. In 1786 Job "paid Captain Meggs two parts in eight parts of a £20 prize in the last State lottery, £5 0 0." In November 1794 he debited the Rev. Sir Harry Trelawny and the Misses Eastcott and their brother with the costs of shares in a lottery ticket. The price of the whole ticket was £16 10s. Thus not only were tickets divided up into shares among various holders; but the most eminently respectable people did not scruple to join in the gamble.

As I have already mentioned, there are many records of women being employed to carry corn on to the boats or to the kilns, e.g. in 1793, 1794, 1798: and I have a note of their employment in 1798 to carry beer on to a boat.

In 1795 Job debited T.S. Eastcott, of Port Looe, "to 11 Jury Men at 1/6 for Dorothy Skinner", i.e. 16s 6d in all; and "to 34 Bearers to carry her to Lansallos Church at 2/6 each, £4 9s 6d" – wherein lay an error of 4s 6d. Here was some tragedy at the plot of which we can only just guess. Obviously the poor woman was a native of Lansallos: and, unless she had been in Eastcott's service, why did the expense fall on him?

In October 1796, Pooley, rector of Lansallos, was debited with sixpence paid "to the Cryer giving notice to gather the fishermen's tithes": and in October 1797 there was another payment of sixpence to the cryer "for publishing the fishermen's tithes". There is a good deal to be said about these tithes later.

On 8th June 1797 there is a very amusing entry: for Sir Harry was debited with 2s paid to William May for "attending at Pelynt to prevent Mayor Chuising". Quite evidently Pelynt had the custom of electing annually a mock mayor: and I infer that the proceeding had become marked by so much disorderliness or worse, that Sir Harry, whether as lord of the manor or as J.P. or in both capacities, determined to suppress this ancient rite. Some relatively important towns in Cornwall – Bodmin and Penryn and Saint Germans – were wont to elect mock mayors, of whose doings there are brief notices in "Nature" of 29th September, and 17th November 1928: but I was astonished to find that such a bit of a village as Pelynt had also the custom. May was probably parish constable: for he was certainly a local official of some kind, as he collected land-tax.

In January 1812, Sir Harry was debited with £1 5s 7¼d "for expence of a militia man charged on the moiety of Henoids (?) Wood in Lanreath". Perhaps this was a billeting charge: but one would like to know whether the occasion was special or not. In January 1819, Job debited Pooley, the absentee rector of Lansallos, with 10s paid to Wm. Toms "to put his daughter, your apprentice girl, to you at Newlyn". Here we come on one of the Lansallos apprentices between No. 56 and No. 63 whose indentures have been lost. Very likely the girl was sister to Thomas Toms apprenticed in 1822. Now under the parish apprenticeship system the poor children, thus provided for, were apprenticed in their own or an adjacent parish and were therefore always in touch with their parents: but, as a result of Pooley's abuse of trust by absenting himself permanently from the rectory which afforded him a comfortable income, this poor child, apprenticed to him as a legal parishioner, was sent away to the other end of Cornwall. There is a lot to be said about Pooley in due course.

With so much prefaced on what may perhaps be considered manners and customs we now come to sheer local history. In No. 26, under date 20th January 1783, I found:- "Agreed with Richard Hobb for 36 feet in Length and 19 feet in Breadth of his Hill next adjoining to my Garden and Paid him 10 and 6 for all his right therein for the remainder of a term of 99 Years detle on 3 lives 10/6". It looks as though we had here an explanation of the name of Hobb's Hill at Crumplehorne in Lansallos parish. To guard against a very natural misunderstanding I may add that Job's garden just mentioned was not part of the Crumplehorne Mill property, which is in Talland parish and was acquired about forty years after Job's death by his great nephew, the late Zephaniah Job.

Let us take in sequence all that is to be said about Job's properties. In 1803 "an orchard near the Mill Leat" was sold for £63, apparently by Thomas "Holting" – i.e. Holten – to Job. In No. 28, under date 3rd March 1801, Job recorded that he "delivered the Key and possession of my New House on the Quay to Mr. Benjamin Rowett and let the House to Him to Keep an Inn therein for – years to commence this day, yearly rent twenty-one pounds". (Job omitted to fill in the blank before "years".) From No. 33 we learn that in March 1812, he "Agreed to reduce the Rent at the year's end which will be 24th June, from £8 p. an. To £4 p. annum Z. Job for the Pier Inn in Polperro Richard Rowett, occupier".

I was interested to learn from an entry of 1804 that "the old Inn at Polperro" was still in commission. I have seen no other reference to this inn, and do not in the least know whether it was identical with the Wheatsheaf of the seventeenth century: and, if this old inn was actually in Polperro village, the name of the well known New Inn is rather curious, since this inn stood, I believe, on what is now and long has been Talland Sands. I wish that the sites of the Old Inn and the Pier Inn and the inn on the quay could be positively identified. I can make a guess at that for the last: but my guess may be wrong.

In December 1782, Job debited the owners of "The Swallow", i.e. John Quiller & Co., "to Jane Quiller for an almanack 9d."

As we have already seen his catholicity extended from thousands of pounds to pence.

Under the date 11th October 1783, I found:- "William Draper, dr., To Cash paid Mr Henry Langmaid for Indemnity for the Parish of Lansallos for his Base Child £10." No doubt Langmaid was warden or overseer: and Draper obviously kept an account with Job. I recollect being puzzled by an entry in the Lansallos registers of the baptism of a child with a very familiar local surname and the Christian names William (?) Draper; but I have no reference at hand. Now I can understand the entry.

On 9th October 1789, Job credited the "Polperro Friendly Society" with £1 18s cash paid in by Samuel Geach: and on 21st January 1790, Geach paid in £2 2s to the credit of the "Polperro Clubb". I am sorry to have found no other record of this society or club: for one would like to know a good deal about its history and functions.

In 1791 Job paid a man 4s 9d for a crown piece – a record which seems to indicate something amiss about the state of the coinage.

There is a curious entry of 1791 or 1792 in No. 20. A very brief account with Mary Warne ends thus. "Paid all her wages in full Z. Job since she married his Excellency Governor Quiller." From the pedigree I find that John Quiller, born 1771, son of John born 1741 and of Jane neé Libby, married Mary Warne: but why he was described as his Excellency Governor Quiller, and whether this was merely some local joke, I do not know. Anyhow his Excellency was uncle to Dr. Couch's second wife.

On 30th October 1795, Job credited Sir Harry Trelawny with 18s per "Joseph Turner for $2/3$ of a six gallon Cask of Brandy taken up on Talland Beach after allowing him $1/3$ for salvage". The meaning is that Sir Harry, as lord of the manor, was legally entitled to all flotsam coming ashore on his manor: but I cannot undertake to say whether the salver took his $1/3$ by law or by custom or by grace.

In October 1796 John Quiller paid £5 5s to the Carpenter family as a "fine for Lease of a Plot of Ground to build a Dwelling House upon".

In October 1807 Job "sent Dr. Rice by Mr.

Jonathan Couch £20". This suggests that Couch may have been in early days assistant or partner to Rice: and, of course, one would like to know how the doctor was related to the Rice who was Job's partner in the timber trade, from 1800 to 1806 at any rate, as we learn from No. 22.

In 1805 J. P. Carpenter and Thomas Phillipps received six guineas "for one year's rent of Nailand Signal Station", and the same in July, 1806, from the Commissioners of the Navy, and the same again in 1807: but in 1810 James Hill's account was credited with three guineas "for rent of the Soil on which the Signal Station standeth". If Couch was correct in giving either 1811 or 1812* as the date at which the manor of Rafiel was sold "by special act" and broken up, it is difficult to understand how Nailand – obviously Nolland's Point – can have passed into Hill's possession before 1810: but on the other hand one doubts whether the Admiralty would have shifted their station from a suitable spot, especially as an account of April, 1808, for half a quarter of coals supplied to Nailand Signal Station, proves that there was some sort of building there and not simply a flag-staff. However, it is of course possible that blundering spendthrifts at the Admiralty were as fond of wasting national money in Polperro at that date as their successors have been during the last forty years.

From various entries we learn that Lansallos parish rented "Colman's House" from the Eastcott family at three guineas yearly "for a Poor's House" – as Job, in common with his contemporaries, correctly describing it in 1787, e.g. instead of using the sloppy vulgarism of "poor house" now and for

---

* on Page 50 of his "History of Polperro" he gives 1811, but on Page 36 he gives 1812 as the date of Sale.

so long in vogue. In 1808 the overseers bought bricks for this house.

In March, 1807, Job paid two guineas to "Monkford for ten weeks' teaching singing in Lansallos Church": and in February, 1809, he paid seven guineas to Thomas Monford "for teaching singing last year at Lansallos, and 3s for strings". These entries suggest that, if the Lansallos records had not been destroyed, there might have been a long story to tell of singing there as at Talland.

We may now take a series of records giving us some information about Polperro harbour which, as included in the manor of Rafiel, belonged to the Carpenter family, or the Carpenter and Phillipps families, until the manor was broken up and the harbour was bought by Job. An entry in March, 1804, acknowledges the subjoined contributions as "received towards the fixing in two Mooring Rings opposite the Outer Quay".

Reginald Barrett & Co. ...	£2 10 6
Chas. Rowett & Co.	£2 10 6
Richard Rowett & Co.	£2 10 6
-- Johns & Co.	£2 10 6
John Rowett & Co.	£2 10 6

The record amuses me much: for I believe that all these people "& Co." were smuggling fraternities – as will appear later. A charge of six guineas, made in this year, for "one year's landlying of a vessel in Polperro Harbour to 10 May last," was misunderstood by me as meaning that the vessel had been laid up for a year occupying harbour room: but sundry examples in 1807 and 1808 prove that "landlying" means landing cargo from vessels. One illustration of

February, 1808, will suffice:- "landlying stones at Mixtow for Lerren Kilns". This is conclusive.

For nine years we have statements of the amounts received for quay dues. In 1803 the dues "received in part" were £8 16s 6d, leaving a balance of £4 2s 6d to be paid in the following year. For 1804 I have discrepant figures of £16 16s 10d and £17 16s 6d: but the former, as entered in the ledger, must be accepted. In May, 1805, there was an obviously special payment of two guineas as quay dues "on fixing out the John Bull privateer".

The figures for the remaining years may be tabulated.

In 1806 ...	£12 10 0	In 1810 ...	£5 4 6
In 1808 ...	£8 4 0	In 1812 ...	£6 4 6
In 1809 ...	£6 18 0	In 1813 ...	£6 2 6

Harbour-owning does not seem to have been a very profitable business.

A loose sheet of paper, preserved by some happy chance, gives us a list of the boat owners in Polperro in 1808-9. I subjoin a verbatim copy.

Polperro Quay dues, Lady-day, 1809.

Owners	Vessels	Due	Received
Rd. Rowett & Co.	Cutter Echo		£1 1 0 received 15 June 1808
			£1 1 0 received 14 July
John Johns & Co.	(illegible)	10/6	10/6
John Jasper	Boat	4/6	- none
Philip Libby	do.	4/6	- con-densed
Thomas Perry	do.	4/6	4/6 not received
John Toms	do.	4/6	4/6
John Pascho	do.	4/6	- condensed?
John Wilcock, sen.	1 do.	4/6	4/6
John Batten	2 do.	9/-	9/-
Zebedee Minards	1 do.	4/6	4/6
John Minards	do.	4/6	4/6
John Wilcock, jun.	do.	4/6	4/6
Robert Hicks	do.	4/6	4/6
Wm. Barrett	do.	4/6	4/6
Henry Langmaid	do.	4/6	4/6
Henry Libby	do.	4/6	4/6 not rec'd
Rd. Oliver jun.	do.	4/6	4/6
Rd. Griffith	do.	4/6	- rec'd afterw'ds 4/6
John Fowler	do.	3/-	3/-
Wm. George	do.	-	-
John Oliver	do.	3/-	3/-
John Rundle	Sand barge	3/-	3/-
Thomas Johns	do.	3/-	3/- not rec'd
P. Littleton	do.	3/-	3/- not rec'd
Polperro Schooner	5 times	5/-	5/-
Other Vessels	-	-	7/-

Since the dues were payable on 25th March, it is obvious that they were incurred to three quarters of the amount in the preceding year. It is clear from comparison of this table with that preceding that Job entered by anticipation four payments as received, and credited these to Carpenter, and then added marginally "not received" for his own guidance. Of the boatmen's names, Griffith was clearly that of some Welsh immigrant: Pascho, Wilcock, Batten and Fowler have disappeared from Polperro more than thirty years ago; and Jasper and Johns have become extinct in the village by death or emigration during the last thirty years. All the other names we still have: but no Minards or Littleton has been a fisherman during these thirty years. In view of what has to be said later about farmers and fishermen, I draw attention to the fact that members of the Oliver and autochthonous Libby families were already on the water.

In 1819 Job debited Phillipps and Carpenter with £100 as "their proportion of rebuilding Polperro outer pier". This rebuilding was necessary to repair the damage wrought by the great storm of 1817, some account of which will be found on p. 34 of Couch's "History of Polperro": but I do not understand why the late owners, if they had sold the harbour seven or eight years previously, were debited with a part of the cost unless by an act of grace on their part.

An entry of January, 1810, affords an incidental illustration of the reaction of war upon such a population as that of Polperro. It concerns the distribution if the effects of the late William Johns, and is as follows. "Mr Reginald Barrett, who married Agas the daughter of the above named William Johns deceased, being in a French Prison Leaving his said Wife and eight small children unprovided for, her Mother, the Widow and Administrator for the deceased William Johns, in consequence of the distress of the family, and for their maintenance and support hath directed me to pay her said daughter Agas Barrett the distribution share of the sum above mentioned, and the said Agas Barrett doth hereby acknowledge the receipt of the same in a/c with Mr Job, and to have received the balance thereof being £137 13s 10d. Witness my hand the 29th January, 1810, Agnes Barrett."

Parenthetically the wonderful feature of this entry is that it is punctuated and, excepting the omission of one comma and the substitution of another for a colon, correctly punctuated. Job seems to have wavered between "Agas" and "Agnes" at the start: for he began with "Agnes" but altered it to "Agas". Richard and Benjamin Rowett had married two other daughters of William Johns who left also sons, John and Richard and Philip. What will, no doubt, puzzle many readers in this entry is the clear implication that the son-in-law was the proper legal heir, while her due share of her father's estate was paid to the daughter only by special act of grace and because her husband – the deceased's son-in-law – could not receive it. The explanation, I think, is that women's rights were then unheard of, and that what should have been a married woman's own property passed automatically to her husband. I noticed that the other two sons-in-law – not their wives – were co-heirs with the sons.

Another sidelight on the wars is afforded by an entry of 1812 that Sir Harry Trelawny gave 30s "to Polperro women to pay a dra (ie draft) of their husbands who are in a French prison".

There is a series of entries in 1815 which I cannot explain, though obviously anyone can make some sort of guess at what history lies behind. On 11th May payments were made to twelve women, wives or mothers of twelve men who, as the next entry tells us, had gone to Newfoundland – ten women receiving two pounds each, and the others ten shillings. It looks as though the payments were made on account of Henry Holdsworth Esq: but this is not certainly clear. On 17th June there is the entry:- "Paid the relatives of men gone to Newfoundland" £21: and on the 13th July:- "Paid the month's half pay to the wives, etc. of men gone to Newfoundland, £20 10s." Similarly in August and September and October there was a payment of £20 10s: but I found nothing later. One supposes that the two whose mothers – presumably – got ten shillings were boys and that one died or returned early: and perhaps all returned after October.

Another series of entries in 1818 and 1819 bears witness to great distress among the fishermen: and it seems to me probable that this distress was the result of that terrible storm on 20th January, 1817, which wrought so much havoc in Polperro. On February, 1818, Job entered £21 from Messrs Carpenter and Phillipps' gift "to the poor fishermen of Polperro": and then followed a record of the distribution of £113 15s "charity money" among eighteen men, of whom two are marked "Looe". In May we find five guineas "charity to Polperro fishermen" from P. W. Mayowe Esq.; and in December "Lord Granville's gift to the poor fishermen of Polperro, £10 10s". In April 1919 there are entries "To poor fishermen, Lord Granville's gift, £10 10s"; and "To ditto, Mrs Wilson's gift, $^1/_3$ of do. £7 7s. N.B. Mr John Richards distributed the other $^2/_3$ to the poor of Talland."

It is a striking fact that I seem to have found no contribution whatever to the starving fishermen from that ecclesiastical scallywag Pooley, the absentee rector of Lansallos, who drew hundreds a year in tithes for doing nothing whatever – as will be shown in due course. If he had merely returned to the fishermen in their distress the total of what he had taken as tithes on fish during his very long incumbency – happy term! – his contribution would have thrown Lord Granville's into the shade. What connection Lord Granville had with Polperro I do not know.

Here this olla podrida may close: for though practically all that has to follow is local history of one kind or another, the records can be grouped into definite sections.

THE TENANTS OF VARIOUS FARMS, etc.

It is of some interest to know who were the tenants of farms and houses over a hundred years ago: and I have been able to collect from Job's books some information that supplements the data afforded by some of the Talland and Lansallos apprenticeship indentures and occasional additions to the wardens' lists. In the sub-joined table – almost confined to farms – I have added in each case a date at which the tenant occupied the farm: but it must be distinctly understood that, with the exception of those cases in which a limiting date is prefixed or added, the tenant may have occupied the farm for years before and/or after that date at which I have happened to find his tenancy mentioned. In the case of Mrs Eastcott's tenants, of whom we have records for several years to 1786, I have guarded against misunderstanding or error by prefixing "before(?)" to the earlier date and "beyond(?)" to the later. So we pass to the table of the farms etc., and their tenants.

Chestlands, Francis Coath, before(?) 1778 to 1784

Chestlands, "Jeales" Collings, 1784 beyond(?) 1786

Colmans, Richard Collings, before(?) 1778 beyond(?) 1786

A field at Crumplehorn, John Quiller and one or two others, September 1787 to 1790

Hendersick, Wm. Harding, 1803 and 1819

High Park, Robert Rean, before(?) 1779

High Park, Richard Parsons, 1797

Lime Kilns, Barrett and Sargent, before 1780 beyond(?) 1786

Longcombe, Francis Coath, before(?) 1776 to November 1785

Longcombe, George Coath, May 1786

Longcombe Mills, George Coath, 1790

Longcombe, Richard Fiddick, 1797 and 1804

"The Island at Looe", John Grigg & Co., 1778

Merrifield, Thomas Jose, 1818

Mortha, Thomas A'Lee, before(?) 1777 to 1784

Mortha, Wm. Sargent, 1784 beyond 1786

New Inn, Hugh Rowe, 1780 to 1786

New Inn, James Roberts and his widow(?) 1786 to 1796

New Inn, Wm. Pearse, 1797

Perglaze, Cornelius Roose, 1807 and 1812

Pigscombe (Pelynt), Cossentine, 1796

Polpever, Joseph Clogg, 1807

Portallow, Thomas A'Lee, 1819

Tregarrick, Wm. Northcott, 1803

*Trelaske, *Wm. Dingle, 1803

Trelaske, Cornelius Roose, 1816

Trelawne Cross House, W. Higgins, before(?) 1778

Trelawne Cross House, sold to Sir H. Trelawney in 1783

Trendaway, Isaac Sargent, 1803
Treweers, John Pollard, before(?) 1778 beyond(?) 1786
Treweers, Nicholas May, 1792 and 1803
Treweers, Fiddick, to 1812
"The Warren etc.", Geo. Collings, before(?) 1778 to March, 1783
"The Warren etc.", Z. Job, March, 1783 beyond(?) 1797
*Wayland, Wm. Dingle, 1803.

All the foregoing were let at what presumably were "rack rents" in the technical sense, i.e. at their market value: but we have the names of a few others which were held by lease on lives at a mere "conventionary" rent plus a small heriot* when one of the lives came to an end. How much "consideration", i.e. premium, had been initially paid to secure the grant of the lease on lives is another matter altogether. We do know, however, not only that a heriot was paid for Gushland in 1797 on the death of James Puckey, but also that Catherine Puckey – presumably his widow – then paid also £320 as "the consideration for adding two lives to one on Gushland". Late in 1819 James Puckey – presumably the son of the former James – paid £5 4s to Job for drawing a grant of Gushland and for stamps. Thus this farm – long since amalgamated with Trendaway – was held by a Puckey family during probably several generations. Again, we know from the payment of heriots in 1796 on Milling Park, and conventionary rents in 1809 on the same and on Lower Botelet and East Polmartin, that these properties were held by that notable smuggler and privateering expert John Quiller. Similarly the payment of a heriot on Millicombe when

---

* a fine (fee) due to the lord of a manor on the death of a tenant

John Grigg died in 1794 renders it probable that the Griggs held this property. I may add that in 1789 William Minard – one would like to know which of the various holders of that name – bought "Polyawna", i.e. evidently Polteana of today, from Sir H. Trelawny: but I much doubt whether the buying was more than the payment of a "consideration" for a grant on lives.

Here it is convenient to explain that the "owners" of various farms included in the foregoing table were not actually the freeholders thereof but merely the lessees at conventionary rents. Thus the Eastcotts paid a conventionary rent to Buller on the New Inn – or its site? – and a "chief" rent, i.e. ground rent, to the Mayor of Looe on the Island House in Looe: and the apparent owner of Portallow paid a conventionary rent to the actual freeholder. However, I did not as a rule extract these particulars: but I was amused to notice how several families were mixed up in this sort of subinfeudation – as one might almost call it.

* * * * *

In the bundle of deeds mentioned at the end of the catalogue there were, as I have said, several "Rentals" of the Manor of Rafiel. It seems fairly obvious that such a rental was drawn up annually in preparation for, or as a sequel to, the Court Leet, so as to bring up to date the list of all the tenants and the description of the holding of each with the conventionary rents and heriots due and the names and ages of those on whose lives the tenancy was held. It will be obvious that any such rental contains a wonderful amount of information of various kinds: and although these manorial tenants were not, I presume, copyholders, yet it seems to me probable that the Master of the Rolls would strongly urge the preservation of these rentals in a public repository with other manorial records. Incidentally I wish that these rentals had been in my hands when I was working at the pedigrees of Polperro and was often badly at a loss to fill in gaps or to clear up ambiguities arising from the duplication or triplication of the same name.

The Rentals of Rafiel thus preserved are those of 1800, 1806, 1808 and 1810: and there are duplicate copies of the first, of which one is partly torn and partly faded from damp and contains various pencilled alterations and additions; while the other copy is in good condition and includes only two or three quite trivial pencilled additions: and some of the "lives" missing in the former are here duly filled in. I provisionally infer that the former copy was made out from the rental of 1799 in readiness for the Court Leet; that the pencilled alterations were made in court; and that the duplicate was a fair copy made out after the court had been held: yet, strangely enough, in occasional instances the bad copy is more up-to-date than the other. I subjoin a transcript of this fair copy, omitting however the less important columns of "Arrears", "Reprises" – i.e. allowances off the rents – "Cash received in Court", "Left unpaid", and usually, "Remarks"; but very occasionally amending it from the bad copy when this latter is clearly more up to date. There are various displacements in the order of tabulation in the fair copy as compared with the bad: but I have followed that of the former. For convenience of reference in the briefest form I have numbered the holdings: but it must be distinctly understood that this numeration is my own and does not occur in the original. It will be noted that in many cases there is a difference of one year between the ages of a "life" on which one tenancy is held and of the same "life" as entered against another tenancy. The explanation is simple and obvious. For example – A. B., whose birthday is in July, takes a lease in March on three lives including his own; he being then over forty years old. Perhaps in September he takes a lease of a second holding on the same lives: but he is now forty-one. Every year at the Court Leet his age is brought up to date on the new Rental, but on the basis of the original entries: and thus the discrepancy is preserved as long as he lives.

I think that all has now been premised which was necessary in order to render the following transcript of the Rental of 1800 intelligible – with the addendum that B. B. as a heriot evidently meant that best beast on the holding: and this is definitely a survival from copyhold tenure.

MANOR OF RAPHIEL CONVENTIONARY RENTS, LADY-DAY, 1800

Tenants	Tenements	Yearly Rent or Dues	Lives	Ages	Heriots
John Baker (1)	Wester East Park	£5 2 0	Richard Baker John, son of Wm. Baker	45 28	£3 6 2
" " (2)	Hole's Tenement	£5 2 0	Thomas Baker John Baker Jane Baker	63 55 49	B.B. or £2 10 0
" " (3)	Landaviddy	£1 16 0	John Baker Jane Baker	55 49	B.B. or £2 0 0
" " (4)	Palaces on the Quay	2/-	John Baker John, his son Catherine, his daughter	55 8 7	4/-

" " (5)	Dwelling House now two	2/-	John Baker	55	6/8
			Jane, his sister	48	
			John Hawkin	24	
Jane Barrett (6)	Manor Hill, Orchard etc.	£1 7 6	John Hawkin	25	£2 0 0
			Jane Barrett	61	
			Jenny, her daughter	40	
Richard Barrett (7)	Above Bakes	4/-	John Hawkin	24	3/-
			Jonathan Couch	11	
			Richard Couch	60	
" " (8)	Part of Stephens' house & garden	6/8	Reginald, his son	36	10/-
			William, his son	27	

Richard Barrett (9)	Saints Hill	5/-	Richard, son of lessee 33 William, ditto 26		10/-
" " (10)	Landaviddy	4/-	Richard Couch Jonathan Couch	61 11	10/-
Richard Barrett (of) Lansallos (11)	Frances' House	5/-	said Richard Barrett William, his son	46 19	4/-
Reginald Barrett (12)	Reginald Barrett House & Garden	3/-	Petronel Sargent Reginald Barrett Agas, his wife	75 28 28	4/-
Reginald Barrett senior (13)	Plot of Ground for Blacksmith's Shop and House	3/-	Reginald Barrett Philippa Barrett Ann Barrett	16 17 13	6/-

Richard Batten (14)	Half Batten's House & Garden	5/-	Joan Batten John, her son	70 41	10/-
Elizabeth Batten (15)	Pearse's House	2/-	said Elizabeth Batten dd. Elizabeth, her daughter	78 47	6/-
Richard Couch (16)	Dwelling House	4/4	Jonathan, his son Mary Rowett Susanna Rowett	12 23 16	6/8
Richard Couch (17)	House & Garden	6/-	said Richard Couch Jonathan, his son Agas Perry, widow	62 12 38	1/-
" " (18)	Dwelling House	6/-	said Richard Couch Philippa, his wife Jonathan, his son	62 57 12	4/-

T. S. Eastcott, Esq. (19)	Couch's House	4/4	said T. S. Eastcott Ann, his sister William Baker	29 26 50	6/8
" " (20)	House, Lime Kiln & Sand-quay	1/-	said T. S. Eastcott Thos. Wilcock Baker John Baker	29 58 56	2/-
Miss Eastcott (21)	Wills's House and Garden	7/-	John Sargent Richard Sargent Susanna Eastcott	36 34 27	10/-
Hugh Fowler (22)	House late Mellows	3/-	Susanna Mellow, now Hutton - William Mellow John, son of lessee	- 22	3/4

" " (23)	late Giddy's House near the Bridge	4/-	Mary Minard John, son of lessee	-	4/-
" " (24)	late Jasper's	2/-	(blank)	-	(blank)
" " (25)	Cragee's House late Richards	2/-	Hugh Fowler Barrett Hugh Fowler, lessee	28 46	2/-
Hugh Fowler (26)	House, Garden & Orchard	5/-	said Hugh Fowler John, his son Charles, his son	46 21 18	4/-
" " (27)	Giddy's House near the Bridge	4/-	(lives as above)	-	½ hundred of Buckhorn

" " (28)	East, alias Adam's Hill	4/-	Richard Barrett 60 John, son of lessee 21 Mary, dr. of Z. Minards 24	10/-
Charles Guy (29)	part of Perry's & Payne's House & Orchard	7/6	said Chas. Guy 61 Martha, his daughter 25 Charles, his son 30	10/-
" " (30)	House, Orchard & Garden	1/-	Elizabeth, dr. of lessee 29 Charles, his son 30 Philippa Quiller 17	2/-
" " (31)	George's alias Pollard's Meadow	2/-	Charles, son of lessee 29 Elizabeth Rowett, dr. of do. 26 Martha Guy, ditto 24	4/-

Name	Property	Rent	Occupants	Age	
Richard Geake (32)	Giddy's Smith's Shop	3/-	said Richard Geake Elizabeth, his wife Elizabeth Sargent	32 37 13	4/-
Margaret Hicks (33)	late Tom's House	3/-	Philippa Toms (blank) Robert, son of lessee Ann, daughter of ditto	35 38	4/-
James Rosse Henna (34)	House & Dockyard	5/-	Lessee Mary, his wife Betsy Ann, their daughter	31 29 7	10/- each
Mary Holton (35)	Wm. Oliver's House, Garden etc.	3/-	Mary Jasper Mary Maynard	51 24	4/-

Name	Description	Ling or 1/-	Lessee / occupants	Age	2/- or 2 lings
Thomas Jasper (36)	(no entry here but "Couch's stable" in dupl..)		Lessee Thomas, his son Elizabeth Perry	80 40 (blank)	
William Jasper (37)	Moiety of Mary Hoskins Premises	3/6	said William Jasper Mary Courtice Susanna Courtice	62 26 15	5/-
William Johns (38)	Walsh's House and Garden	5/-	Philippa, wife of lessee William, his son Rd. Oliver Johns, grandson 8½	58 30	10/-
" " (39)	Dwelling House late Code's	7/-	Phillis Rowett, dr. of lessee Rd. Johns, his son P. L. Johns	28 17 14	14/-

Name	Property	Rate	Occupants	Ages	Amount
William Johns (of Lansallos) (40)	House & Garden	4/4	said Wm. Johns Mary, his wife Richard Rundle	60 55 30	6/8
Z. Job (41)	Cornelius Martin's House	6/-	said Z. Job Z. Job, junior John Andrews	48 30 32	8/-
Widow of R. Rowett (42)	Dwelling House etc.	2/-	Z. Job (see note) Z. Job, his nephew Wm. Andrew	48 30 25	4/-
Sarah Langmaid (43)	Jewtorne Park	6/4	Priscilla Libby Thomas, son of lessee Samuel, son of lessee	54 25 23	£1 0 0

" " (44)	Lannear late Mellows	£1 6 0	John Johns 40 Cornelius Roose, jun. 24 John, son of Thos. Johns 24	(blank)
" " (45)	Moiety of late Hoskin's House	3/6	John Langmaid 71 said Sarah Langmaid 56 Samuel, her son 22	5/-
John Langmaid (46)	Cellars and Chamber over	2/-	said John Langmaid 75 Catherine, his wife 68	4/-
" " (47)	Part of Giddy's House, Cellar & Bakehouse	2/6	said John Langmaid 75 Catherine, his wife 68 Mary, dr. of Richard Batten now Rickard 47	(blank)

Lessee	Property	Rent	Lives	Ages	Heriot
John Langmaid jun. (48)	Undertown in Landaviddy	5/6	Cecilia, wife of lessee John, his son Thos., his son in reversion	39 7 2	12/-
" " (49)	Dwelling House etc.	6/-	said John Langmaid Ruth, his sister Wm., his son, in reversion	30 25 6	10/-
Philip Libby (50)	Couch's House	6/-	Priscilla Libby Ann, daughter of lessee Thos. Holting, in reversion	55 38 31	5/-
" " (51)	Orchard and two willow gardens formerly granted with Jewstorne Park	2/-	Priscilla Libby Sarah Libby Thomas Holten	55 20 11	10/-

Wm. Minard (52)	George's or Barrett's House	4/-	Lessee Jane, his wife Mary, their daughter	35 41 13	5/-
Johanna Minard (53)	late Ann Taprell's	4/-	said Johanna Minard John, her son Wm., her son, in reversion	40 20 17	5/-
Zebedee Minards (54)	House & Garden late Jane Minards	5/-	said Zebedee Minards Mary Minards	61 66	5/-
" " (55)	New House on the Quay near Rommetts	5/-	Mary Minards said Zebedee Minards Mary, his daughter	66 61 26	10/-

Thos. Mark (56)	Moiety of Batten's House & Garden	5/-	said Thos. Mark Susanna, his wife Susanna, their daughter	60 60 33	10/-
John Mark (57)	House & Garden	1/4	Jane, wife of lessee John, their son Thomasine, their daughter	61 31 29	(blank)
Richard Mutton (58)	House & Garden Part of Manor Mill Tenement	2/-	said Richard Mutton Catherine, his wife Tammy, their daughter	41 40 14	4/-
Richard Oliver (59)	late John Oliver's	5/-	said Richard Oliver Margaret, his wife Sarah, the wife of Richard Oliver, in reversion	61 55 26	10 ling or 10/-

" " (60)	Part of Silvester Perry's	5/-	Mary Perry John, son of lessee Mary Perry	43 33 41	4/-
Reginald Barrett (61)	Dwelling House etc., late Philly Pincent	3/-	Jenefor Robins Agnes Barrett Mary Clogg	12 6 24	4/-
Thos. Pinsents Exors. (with marginal note "now Nathaniel Hearle and Antony Jeeves") (62)	East Park, Ball Park and North Hill	12/-	Robert Thomas Stephen Puddicombe, jun. 27	28	6/8
ditto ditto (63)	Above Bake's, East Hill & Willow Garden	5/-	Same lives	-	5/-

Thos. Pinsent's Exors. (with marginal note "Regd. Barrett") (64)	Palace on Outer Quay	6/-	Richard Barrett Reginald Barrett Mary Barrett, now wife of Arthur Martin	46 37 38	10/-
Thos. Pinsent's Exors. (with marginal note "Nathaniel Hearle" erased in pencil and "Puddicombe" pencilled in.) (65)	½ East Hill late Rowett's	3/-	John Rommett Rowett Catherine Rowett	24 20	5/-
Elizabeth Perry (66)	House & Orchard	5/-	Jane, wife of H. Jasper Elizabeth Perry	(blank) 43	10/-

Mary Pearse (67)	late Jasper and Burrows	5/-	James Pearse said Mary Pearse Richard, her son	56 56 26	4/-
James Pearse (68)	Cottage & Garden	6/-	Ann, lessee's daughter Jenny, lessee's daughter Susan, lessee's daughter	15 14 12	5/-
" " (69)	Old Palace with Cellar at Kit's Hill House	4/-	Lessee Ann, his wife Elizabeth his daughter	40 40 17	4/8
John Quiller (70)	late Tom's	8/-	Z. Job, jun. Thomas Toms Philippa Toms, now Solomon	30 33 30	12/-

" " (71)	Warren's House and Orchard	5/4	Mary Quiller, in reversion of Mary Roskilly Wm. Quiller	39 67 33	3/4
Wm. Quiller (72)	Part of Lawrence Tom's House, etc.	3/-	Phillis Quiller, his wife Phillis, his daughter Elizabeth, his daughter	35 15 13	6/-
Richard Rickard (73)	Part of Malthouse on the Green	4/5	Henry, lessee's son Richard, ditto	39 37	4/5
Ann Rickard (74)	The other part of ditto	2/3	said Ann Rickard Jane Johns	74 45	2/3

[The bad copy erases Ann and adds in pencil Thomas Johns 24, Ezekiel Johns 17 in reversion]

Charles Rowett [see note later re changes here] (75)	late Lawrence Tom's House	4/4	Chas. Rowett Martha, his wife Susanna, their daughter	26 25 1½	10/-
Richard Rowett's exors. (76)	late Gilbert's	3/-	Ann Rowett Henry Stivey	53 54	2/-
" " (77)	New House on the Green	5/-	Ann Rowett Ann, her daughter	52 24	10/-
Benjamin Rowett (78)	Part of Lawrence Tom's House	5/-	Lessee Mary, his wife Mary, their daughter	37 26 6½	(blank)

Name (No.)	Property		Occupants	Ages	
Thos. Toms (79)	Moors (and) Sprights	6/-	said Thomas Toms Phil, his wife	55 55	8/-
John Toms (80)	Jane's House	6/-	Edith Johns Lessee Jane, his wife	26? 32 36	8/-
Catherine Toms (81)	late Phillipps' House & Garden	6/-	said Catherine Toms Dorothy, her daughter	70 31	8/-
John Taprill (82)	his late father's House & Garden	6/-	said John Taprill Elizabeth, his wife Margaret Rundle	63 70 42	5/-
Edward Soady (83)	House near higher bridge	3/-	said Edward Soady Edward, his son John Willcock	37 13 (blank)	5/-

John Willcock (84)	New House on the Green	5/-	Lessee	26
			Elizabeth, his wife in reversion	26
			Elizabeth Rundle	29	10/-
David Thompson (85)	Part of Stephen's House	3/4	(No entries in either copy)	
William Quiller (86)	Meadow Dorothy Marks'	2/-	Lessee	33
			Phillis, his wife	34
			Elizabeth, their daughter	12	5/-

MANOR OF RAPHIEL FREEHOLDS AT RACK RENTS, 1800

Lease	Tenants	Term	Commencing	Yearly Rent
2 Novr. 1784	James Hill	Barton of Raphiel West Hill and New Park	21 years Lady-day, 1784	£70 0 0
1 Decr. 1797	James Pearse	Higher & Lower Posgreens and Cunroys	14 years Lady-day, 1798	£40 0 0
No Date	Saml. Sargent	Higher Quary	at will Michaelmas	£1 0 0

(There are also particulars which I did not extract of the rack-rented "Western Scattered Lands", five in all, situated in Bodmin, St. Winnow, Lanhydrock, Cardinham and Landlevery)

The Conventionary Rents received in 1800 amounted to £30 1s – none being left unpaid. The amount, of course, was trivial: but we know nothing as to the initial payment – the "consideration" – on the grant of a lease or on the addition of fresh lives. The whole system was iniquitous and improvident – apart from the fact that it was a gamble between landowner and tenants, i.e. a gamble on the duration of the "lives". The landowner, if he had luck, might find nearly all the tenancies fall in during his life ownership, and he could thus pocket altogether a large sum as "considerations" for new grants, while his son or other successor in the manorial lordship might get little or nothing but the annual conventionary rents, such as they were, if at least one life on each tenement outlasted his own. It was a system which mortgaged the future to the greed or needs of the moment.

Some few additional remarks are now necessary on certain differences between the two copies of the 1800 Rental. After No. 24 in the bad copy there is a pencilled note that James Hill and James Pearce (apparently) have each of them one of Fowler's tenements. If we had the Rental of 1801 we should, no doubt, find the relevant alterations. In No. 35 of the bad copy Mary Jasper's name is crossed through and there is the pencilled addition of "Mary lessee's wife, 21, John, his son, in reversion". In this case the bad copy is clearly more up to date. In No. 36 all the "lives" are crossed through in the bad copy which also alone tells us what the tenement was: and it will be found that the 1806 Rental clears up matters. No. 42 in the bad copy is assigned to Job; but there is a pencilled alteration to the widow of R. Rowett: and naturally the first life is entered as "lessee" in this copy. No. 46 is assigned to

Robert Hicks in the bad copy: but the lives column is blank. The fair copy has the marginal note: "Robert Hicks. Enter the new lives." Of No. 50 I may note that in the bad copy Philip's name is spelled Libbey in the old way. Philip was a typical name of the autochthonous family. At the bottom of this page is a pencilled note assigning Soady's house to Samuel Langmaid. After No. 69 the bad copy gives in pencil a third tenement to James Pearse, namely "Dwelling house, new built, one of Douster's(?)": but no dues or lives are entered. I could not trace this on the fair copy; and I cannot opine whether his third tenement in 1806 was this house. There seems to have been a good deal of complication about No. 75. In the fair copy it had been entered to Jane Rowett's executors on the lives of Phillis Rowett aged 50 and John Rowett aged 33, with a heriot of 6s 8d: but the entry had been erased and replaced by Jane Rommett's executors; the two old "lives" had been crossed off; and a marginal note had been added: "Now leased to Chas. Rowett. Enter the new lives". In the bad copy the new lives are entered: but the tenancy remains assigned to Jane Rommett's executors. In this case I accepted the indication of the marginal note, and entered Charles Rowett as tenant. It is curious that there were – as I already knew – both Rommetts and Rowetts in Polperro, and that the two families intermarried: and the addition of "daur" to Phillis Rowett's name suggests that she was Jane Rommett's daughter. The complications and apparent contradictions about No. 75 in the later rentals so bewildered me that eventually I made a long comparative re-examination with the following result. Either two tenements – "late Lawrence Toms'" and "late Rommett's" – were somehow confused in 1800; or the one tenement was divided into two, viz: into (1) "late Lawrence Toms'" which was let to Richard Rowett (who was possibly husband of Phillis and died before 1800) on the old lines of Phillis and John, at 4s 4d rent and dues but no heriot; and (2) "late Rommett's" which went to Charles Rowett at 5s rent and 10s heriot on his own and Martha's and Susanna's lines. I shall refer to this as No. 75a. The striking fact that no heriot was payable henceforth on No. 75 is perhaps evidence for the division of one tenement into two.

In the 1806 Rental there are the following changes. No. 4 is marked as "sold to Z. Job, John Mark and John Wilcock": but of course they had bought only the tenancy – not the freehold. To No. 6 there is the note: - "N.B. – 5 new houses are built on this tenement." Richard Barrett's executors are now entered for Nos. 7 to 10; and Jane Barrett of Lansallos replaces her husband – as one infers – in No. 11 with the addition of two new "lives", namely, herself aged 49 and Richard Barrett aged 17. No. 13 has just passed from Reginald Barrett senior to James Trehane, whose name is written in over Barrett's, but the "lives" are the same. We next come to difficulties of identification which are accentuated, indeed rendered hopeless, by some disturbance in the order of sequence. Immediately following No. 15 we find John Billing as tenant of a dwelling house, at a rent of 4s and dues of one ling or 2s, and a heriot of 10s, on the lives of the lessee and his wife Martha and their son Robert John, aged respectively 34 and 31 and 4. This may have been, and probably was, one of the houses mentioned below as no longer held by the tenants of 1800: but I cannot identify it. Then follows No. 19 which is entered to Wm. Braddon on the original lives and at the same rent, but with the note that "the rent is 6s: Hutton to pay 4s, Parish of Lansallos 2s: Littleton has also a part of this house and pays nothing".

Then follows Nos. 16, 17, 18; and then the entry of a tenement to Ben Coad, at 4s rent and 2s heriot, on the lives of himself and his wife Honour (thus mis-spelled) and Robert Jeffery, aged respectively 44 and 44 and 17. This house also I cannot identify. Hugh Fowler no longer has Nos. 22, 25 and 27; and poor Henna – of whom later – is out of 34: but although we thus have four houses available for new tenants, they all have descriptive names by which they should at once be identified. For No. 46 Hicks is tenant of a dwelling house, at 2s with no heriot, on the lives of himself and his wife Mary and their son Robert, aged respectively 41 and 42 and 14: and next comes William Hacken (Hocken) as tenant of a new built house, at 5s rent and 5s heriot, on the lives of his sons John and William and Edward, aged respectively 29 and 26 and 17. Once more I cannot identify Hocken's house.

We now get back to the 1800 order and find that John Jasper has succeeded Thomas in No. 36, that the tenement is now a "dwelling house formerly a stable", with no rent but one ling as dues, on the lives of himself and his wife Mary – now dead – and his daughter Edith, aged 46 and 38 and 15 respectively. I take this opportunity of noting that the 1806 Rental differs from that of 1800 by including in a large number of cases – actually in over a third of them – dues in ling or money as well as rent. Subject to legal correction I infer that all dues and rents in kind – which would naturally be fish at Polperro – were definite survivals from genuine copyhold tenure.

Our course continues smoothly in the 1800 order for most of the way now. William Johns is succeeded by his executors in Nos. 38 and 39: Sarah Langmaid is out of No. 44, which is entered – but next after No. 60 – to John Oliver on the original lives and still with no heriot: Catherine Langmaid has succeeded her husband in Nos. 46 and 47: Philip Libby no longer has No. 51: William Minard is succeeded by his executors in No. 52, and John Mark by his widow in No. 57: and John Perry now replaces Elizabeth in No. 66, on the lives of Elizabeth Perry and John Perry and his wife Ann, aged respectively 49 and 27 and 28 – these second and third lives having been added since 1800. Our old friend John Clements the arithmetician now has No. 70 in lieu of John Quiller's executors and on the original lives: Catherine Toms is succeeded in No. 81 by her executors: and Samuel Langmaid replaces Soady in No. 83 in accordance with the intercalation of 1800 – this tenement, however, now following next after No. 49.

Richard Rowett's executors are entered for No. 75: while No. 75a is still held by Charles Rowett, who has also a "new house". For No. 85 we now have the lives of David Thompson and Mary, his wife: but the ages are not given.

We now again come to difficulties which I have reserved for consideration en masse. James Pearse has, in addition to Nos. 68 and 69, a third house "late Jenny Bunt's" at 5s rent with 2s heriot on the lives of his sons William and James and John, aged respectively 14 and 11 and 9. As the 1800 Rental included neither Jenny Bunt as a tenant nor any house described as "late Jenny Bunt's", we cannot identify it. Possibly this house, and several others which cannot be identified, were vacant in 1800: and anyhow the description and rent do not fit any of the tenements Nos. 22 to 28 of which Pearse had apparently just taken one in 1800. Again, next after Charles we find William Rowett as tenant of a house and shipwright's yard, at 5s rent and 10s heriot, on the lives of himself "d.d." – presumably deceased – and his wife Elizabeth and their son William aged 32 and 32 and 10; and as tenant also of a new house and plot in front at 5s rent and 5s heriot, on the first and second of these lives and on that of his son, Charles, aged 8½. The house and shipwright's yard are pretty clearly No. 34: but the "new house" may well have been built since 1800. Finally Richard Rowett – but there were so many Richard Rowetts in the roll call of Polperro – follows with a house, at 2s rent but no heriot, on the lives of his children Ann and Richard and Joseph aged respectively 15 and 12 and 9: and this house cannot be identified.

It will already have become clear that these rentals constitute, inter alia, a register of births and marriages and deaths. If all such Rentals of all manors for every year throughout the centuries had been preserved, genealogists would have a mass of data often far more valuable than those – so often hopelessly useless – in church registers; because in these manorial rolls one can trace ages at marriage and can often determine which of various Richard Rowetts or Samuel Langmaids or Richard Barretts was the son of which among several seniors having the same name as his own. When writing on the Pedigrees of Polperro, I explained the criminal shortcomings of church registers in these respects.

The changes in the Rack-rents can be stated very briefly. James Hill has a fresh lease for fourteen years at the increased rent of £105 yearly: Michael Hickey is now co-tenant with Sargent of Higher Quarry at two guineas instead of one: John Congdon has another quarry at a guinea: Richard Mutton and Robert Fowler have a third at two guineas: and John Andrew has a garden at one and a half guineas.

It is worth noting that against the eighty-six tenements at conventionary rents in 1800 there were ninety in 1806, ninety-four in 1808, and ninety-five in 180. These additions account for some of the difficulties of identification already discussed.

*   *   *   *   *

The changes in the Rental of 1808 will not detain us long. The second Jane Barrett of No. 11 now has also "part of Toms" house at 4s rent and 8s heriot on the lives of William and Richard and John Barrett aged respectively 28 and 21 and 16. It is difficult to identify this house simply as Toms', since several were named after Toms in 1800. Trehane's tenement No. 13 is now described as a house late a smith's shop: and in No. 19 Braddon is replaced by Hutton at 4s while the Parish still pays 2s – but this does not necessarily imply that Braddon had ceased to occupy the house at Hutton's and the parishioners' expense. Some little bit of local history is just indicated here. Job has two fresh tenements, namely (1) a new stable at 5s rent and 5s heriot, on the lives of Jonathan Couch and Henry Tregare junior and Charles Guy jun. aged respectively 10 and 13 and 5; and (2) "part of Toms' garden", at 2s rent, on the lives given above for No. 70 of which this was no doubt a part. The new stable we cannot expect to identify, if it was really wholly new. It is amusing to note how Job picked out sound young lives: and as at least one of the three, namely that of Jonathan Couch, lasted until 1870, his judgement was fully justified by the event.

To continue - John Langmaid junior, of Nos. 48 and 49, has now a third tenement, namely part of Toms' house on which the life of Philippa Toms, aged 63, along survives. Apparently therefore this tenement was part of No. 33; although the omission of Philippa's age in 1800 leaves us just short of certainty. Next after No. 50 comes a new John Mark as tenant of No. 4 – now a "house on the quay" – on the original Baker lives. Richard Rowett's executors have disappeared: and in their place Thomas Rowett has No. 76, and John Parkin has No. 77 in both cases on the old lives, while Martha Rowett, obviously the widow of Charles, has No. 75. The house of Richard Rowett of 1806 is marked "in ruins": William Rowett, of the same year, equally with Charles, is now replaced by his executors: and Thomas Toms is now in possession of No. 81.

In the Rack-rent list Hickey alone has the Higher Quarry; while Fowler and Mutton and Andrew have disappeared. As already in 1806 the error of "Posgreens" is replaced by "Polgrains".

The 1810 Rental can be disposed of as quickly as the former. The original Jane Barrett of No. 6 is now replaced by her executors: and No. 7 is now properly described as "a field called above Bakes". In No. 20 two limekilns are specified: and herein lies the proof, already mentioned, that Eastcott still held the Polperro kilns in 1`810. No. 32 – with the old description of "Giddy's smith's shop" crossed through, and "Dwelling House" written above – is now held on the Geake lives by "John Minards (Green)"; but whether he was nicknamed "Green" or had lived on the Green, we do not know. Curiously, the rent is 2s instead of 3s. No. 46 is followed by an insertion noting that William Hodge has a dwelling house with garden in front:

but the rent and the "lives" had not been entered. Evidently he had only just been admitted. William Johns' executors are replaced by Mrs Johns's executors in No. 38 and by Philip Johns in No. 39. Job's additional holding of 1808, part of No. 70, as it appeared, is now described as a house and part of a garden, etc: And Sarah Langmaid has all Hoskin's house, i.e. presumably No. 37 as well as No. 45. Samuel Langmaid is replaced in No. 83 by John Oliver – still on the Soady lives – and Thomas Mark has all Battens, i.e. presumably No. 14, as well as No. 56. William Quiller of No. 86 now has not only Dorothy Marks' meadow but also her, or a, house therewith: and Jane Johns replaces her mother Ann Rickard in No. 74. Charles Rowett's executors have disappeared and are replaced by Martha Rowett in the "New House" and in No. 75a: and William Rowett's executors give place to Elizabeth Rowett in No. 34 and the "New house": while William Johns now has David Thompson's house, No. 85, on the original lives.

Below the list of Rack-rents is a note that Samuel Sargent has little Raphiel, at a conventionary rent of £2 6s 6d and a heriot of £4, on the lives of Robert Rean and his wife Sarah and his daughter Ann, aged respectively 41 and 38 and 20. Incidentally Hocken's name is spelled correctly in this Rental – which must have been very nearly the last Rental of Raphiel or Rafiel compiled, since the manor was broken up and sold a year or two later.

I think anyone who studies my transcript of the 1800 Rental, and realises that a similar document must have been compiled every year, will agree that Job's services as a steward would not have been overpaid if he had done nothing else – instead of much else – for his five guineas yearly. I speak feelingly and from experience: for this section has cost me many many hours of labour and strained attention.

ADDENDUM ON RAPHIEL MANOR

Just as the transcript of the 1800 Rental was in the Press I discovered an additional document that I now subjoin. It is endorsed "Heriots due. Manors of Raphiel and Lansallos." There is no date: but from comparison with the 1800 Rental it is clear that this list belongs to a somewhat earlier year, possibly to 1799 or 1798. I was very interested to find that the tenements here were numbered. The numbers of many are the same as those (supplied by me) in the fair copy of 1800; while the rest – with two exceptions – differ by only one unit: but one has no clue to the changes that brought (73) and (74) into accord with 73 and 74, but turned 78 into (77). The motive for shifting 37 to (80) was apparently the desire to put the three Toms family's tenements together, though held by three different members of the family. No. 88 is a puzzle: for it seems to duplicate 7 which is the same as (7). It is very obvious that these Rentals would have been far more valuable if each tenement had been numbered unalterably. It will be noticed that this list includes just one entry referring to the Manor of Lansallos – of which I have found no rental.

I have added in brackets at the right of the subjoined list the number according to the Rental of 1800.

No.	Tenants	Tenements	Due (No.)

LANSALLOS MANOR

No.	Tenants	Tenements	Due (No.)
9	Robert Rean	Tregavissick, on the Death of Elizabeth his sister	(blank)

RAPHIEL MANOR

No.	Tenants	Tenements	Due (No.)
7	Richard Barrett	Bove Bakes, on the Death of Matthew his son	3/- (7)
8	Richard Barrett	Stephen's House and Garden on the Death of Jane his daughter	10/- (8)
	Ditto	Landaviddy, on the Death of Matthew his son	10/- (10)
11	Richard Barrett of Lansallos	Frances' House on the Death of Jane his wife	4/- (11)
23	Hugh Fowler	Late Giddy's House near the Bridge on the Death of Jane Rummett	4/- (23)
25	Ditto	Cragoe's House on the Death of Elizabeth Fowler	2/- (25)
34	Mary Holten	Oliver's House, Garden and Orchard on Death of Elizabeth Johns	4/- (35)
37	Francis Johns	Jane's House on the Death of Mary Jasper	8/- (80)
		Ditto – death of Joan Pearce	8/-
46	John Langmaid	Cellar & Chamber – Death of Ann his sister	4/- (46)

48	John Langmaid	Undertown in Landaviddy – Death of Wm. Oliver	12/-	(48)
49	Ditto	Dwelling Houses etc. Death of ditto	10/-	(49)
53	Wm. Maynard	George's or Barrett's House – death of Grace Barrett	2/-	(52)
60	Richd. Oliver	Late John Oliver's – Death of Wm. Oliver	10/-	(59)
62	Philly Pinsent	Maynard's House – Death of Thos. Pinsent	4/-	(61)
63	Thos. Pinsent's executors	East park, Ball Park & Northill - Death of said T. Pinsent	6/8	(62)
	Thos. Pinsent's executors	Above Bake's East Hill and Willow Garden – Death of said Thos. Pinsent	5/-	(63)
66	Ditto	Moiety of East Hill – Death of John Rowett	5/-	(65)
73	Richard Rickard	Part of the Malt House on ye Green. Death of said Richard Rickard	4/5	(73)
74	Ann Rickard	The other part of ditto – Death of Ezekiel, her son	2/3	(74)
78	Richard Rowett's executors	New House on the Green - Death of Richard Rowett	10/-	(77)
88	Rd. Barrett	Bove Bakes – Death of Matthew his son.	3/-	(7)

It may be noticed that in 23 we have "Rummett" instead of Rommett; that in 25 and 34 respectively the names of Cragoe and Holten are spelled correctly instead of as Cragee and Holton in 1800; and that in 53 and 62 there is the original form – as I believe it to be – of Maynard instead of Minard. From 62 (61) we can learn how the names of the houses changed. As long as "Philly" Pinsent lived in this house it was called "Maynard's House" – evidently from her predecessor: but, when she was succeeded by a new tenant, the house became "late Philly Pincent's" (with no uniformity of spelling either) as in 1800.

LOCAL ARTIZANS AND CRAFTSMEN
AND OTHERS

To those who live in a small community and know the occupations of all their neighbours it is a matter of interest to learn who were the farmers and carpenters and masons and so on of the past: and any such information may at any time prove of considerable value in certain departments of social enquiry. I have already listed the names of a large number of farmers in my accounts of the Records of Talland and Lansallos; and in the foregoing pages additions have been made to the list, and the names noted of various fishermen of the first decade of the nineteenth century: and I now proceed to give the names of a number of men following various occupations between 1779 and 1812. Incidentally the list includes several surnames not previously recorded for Polperro: and, as I pointed out when dealing with the Records of Lansallos, it is very desirable to preserve as complete a list as possible of all the surnames that have been current in each district in the past. It will be observed that certain names in the subjoined list are asterisked. These, with others, were taken from No. 14, which, as I have said, serves as a sort of local trade directory: but, as no address is given to anyone whose name is thus asterisked, I am uncertain whether such lived in Polperro or in one of the neighbouring parishes. At first I thought that the absence of any address indicated residence in Polperro: but the test proved inconclusive, because the addresses of some Polperro men are given, whilst in some cases no addresses are given of men who certainly lived elsewhere. There are various names on which comment will be necessary: but the names must precede the comments. Here then is the list:

Agricultural labourers (additional to those mentioned in the section on wages): William Coath, George Fiddick, William Hambly, Luke Leatherby, Henry Tregaire (all employed by Job).

Auctioneer: John Littleton.

Carpenters: John Andrew, *Thomas Angear, *James Congdon, John Conning, John Cossentine, William Geach (cooper), *John Harding, Matthew Hawken, *Henry Heal, Richard Hocking (cooper), John Hore (joiner), *Richard Luke, Joseph Mitchell, - Pearn, John Rickard (joiner), John Rendle (cooper), *Samuel Slade sen., John Wilcock (shipwright).

Glazier: Samuel Ellis.

Grocer: Pitherick Lukey.

"Lime burner at Polperro" William Higgins. Ditto, (where?) George Teague.

Masons: John Congdon, Michael Hickey, William Hill, Hodge (apparently), John Hole, William Ough, Thomas Pinch, Thomas Rendle, Josephus Sargent, Samuel Sargent, Edward Soady, -- Tozer.

Shoemakers: Walter Pascoe, John Perry (apparently).

Sadler: -- Geach.

Smiths: Richard Libby, Richard Oliver, William Pearse, William Puckey (alias Pukey), George Teague, James Truscott.

Tailor: Philip Littleton.

"Tidsman" (? Harbour-master?) Philip Libby.

I have noted also the following in neighbouring parishes.

Richard Bolling, carpenter, Pelynt.
Richard Libbey, cabinet maker, Liskeard.
Richard Rawling, carpenter, Pelynt.
John Waynhall, carpenter, East Looe.

I have not included in the list of Polperro names those of Samuel Stone and Philip Moysey, who supplied bread to a Polperro privateer, because I could find no certain proof that the bread was supplied at Polperro and not at some other port at which the privateer may have put in ; but they may have been Polperro bakers. I have also not included the name of John Vanderslys alias Vandersluys, alias Vandersluce, obviously the "Vandersling" whose name as a witness on a Lansallos apprenticeship indenture of 1791 so puzzled me. I then hazarded the suggestion that he was a magistrate's clerk; but sundry entries in Job's books prove that he was a bookseller. It is scarcely conceivable, however, that anyone could have made even a scantiest living by selling books at Polperro during the latter half of the eighteenth century: and since Job paid Vandersluys for books supplied to Mrs Eastvott and Pooley – both of whom lived at Lostwithiel – I think it probable that Vandersluys' shop was at Lostwithiel. Since he was probably well known by various Polperro people, he could very well function when a witness to a signature was required because, perhaps, the signature and attestation had been neglected at Polperro, and it was necessary to put things in order at once for the magistrates.

I must add that in 1787 Job debited Mrs Eastcott's executors with 15s "to Vandersluce – bill for dancing". This seems to indicate that our bookseller was also a dancing-master.

Now let us consider some of the names on this list, and first of all those asterisked. I have been overscrupulous, perhaps, in thus marking Angear and Congdon and Harding and Slade, since these were Talland or Lansallos names: but I have no positive proof that any one of these four individuals did not live in Looe or Pelynt. The surname Luke also occurs in the Lansallos Records: but this does not prove that Luke the carpenter lived in Polperro. Still, as a result of this examination, Heal alone among the six asterisked can at all confidently be presumed to have lived in some neighbouring parish. As regards two others in the list of carpenters, I cannot prove that Geach lived in Polperro and not in Looe: but Geach was an old Polperro name; and we have already found a Samuel Geach in the village at this period: and I thought that Hawken was probably a Polperro man. As to Ellis the glazier – wherever he lived he was working on a house in Polperro with Ough and Rickard and other Polperro men. I feel some doubt about the saddler Geach simply because it seems doubtful whether there would have been a saddler in such a village. I may be mistaken: or he may have been a Polperro man who had migrated to Looe. Anyhow Job paid Geach's bills on behalf of his clients.

I draw attention to the names of Coath and Fiddick in the list of farm labourers, because these were also the names of farmers. Here again then we may have examples of very different status in the same family.

William Puckey, the smith, puzzled me, because he evidently is not included in the Puckey pedigrees that I was able to draw up. William born in 1764 could scarcely have already been a smith in 1781: and the other William, ancestor of one of the two lines of Puckeys in Polperro, was not born until years after 1781.

Since I have noted the use made of No. 14 in this section, I will add that it gives Liskeard as the address of Cornelius Quiller in 1789. This must have been – as I infer – the Cornelius who was born in 1738 and had three children baptized at Lansallos, where also his grandson Cornelius was baptized in 1781. I should much like to know whether the Liskeard Quillers can trace their descent from Cornelius or not.

I should add in conclusion (1) that Wynhall the carpenter of Looe was evidently the "Mr John Winall" who put up the gallery in Talland Church in 1775-78; (2) that Zebedee Minards was still in evidence in 1820, as he had been a generation earlier in Job's books, as the one purveyor of fish to the neighbourhood – or at any rate to Job's circle; and (3) that I have intentionally omitted various unfamiliar names of labourers working on the quay in 1817 because I suspect that they were strangers temporarily working here.

FISHING AND FARMING FAMILIES.

In my account of the Records of Lansallos I quoted the late Dr. Guppy's opinion that fisher families, if traced far enough back, would be found to be descended from farmers: and I admitted that my unexpected discoveries in those records that William Oliver and Cornelius Roose were farmers had much shaken my own earlier belief that fisher families had been segregated for centuries from the rest of the population. I have now to point out that a series of entries in Job's book affords additional and striking support to Dr. Guppy's contention and seems to render my own suggestion untenable – at least so far as Polperro is concerned. Most of this new evidence has already been indicated more or less incidentally in my accounts of the lime business and corn trade and in the section dealing with the tenants of farms: but it is necessary now to present it in connected form.

There are altogether four fresh families concerned, i.e. four additionally to those discussed in the Records of Lansallos. I have already noted that William Courtis spent £5 10s on lime in 1796, and bought 56lbs of clover seeds from Poole in 1791: that John Cortis spent £4 on lime in 1801; and that both William and John sold corn to Job and Grigg. I have now to add that in 1780 and onwards William Courtice appears in the list of tithe-payers in Lansallos, and that at least as early as 1782 John Cortice – for they rang the changes on the spelling of this surname! – also appears in this list. Finally I have found in the packet of deeds mentioned at the end of the catalogue a deed of assignment by Robert Thomas of Lanteglos, yeoman, to William Courtis of Lansallos, yeoman, of the lease of North Tregue for the remainder of the term of a lease for twenty-one years granted to Thomas in September, 1795, by Francis Howell at £30 yearly.

Now in "The Pedigrees of Polperro" I noted that the existing Curtis clan of Polperro "is wholly descended from one man born not 150 years ago, namely from one William born in 1767". It is clear that the William who was paying tithes as early as 1780 was not the man born in 1767: but the latter may well have been the son of the farmer of Tregue. I have no longer the Curtis pedigree at hand and cannot remember whether the William of 1767 was the son of a William. If he was, then our farmer William was presumably himself the ancestor of the whole existing clan: but anyhow there is the certain fact that less than 150 years ago there were two farmers in a family that is now, and for long has been, typically and almost wholly a fishing family.

Again I find that in 1780, 1781, and so on, Thomas Marks was paying tithes in Lansallos parish: and, although I have no note of the purchase of any quantity of lime or sale of corn by him, yet the inference from his tithe-paying is certainly that he was a farmer. Moreover the William Marks, who spent over £10 on lime in 1796 and £5 14s 9d in 1806, must obviously have been a farmer: whereas one has been accustomed to think of this family also as a family of seamen and fishermen.

In the Toms family the evidence for farming is very definite. Not only did Nathaniel Toms buy lime to the value of nearly £15 in 1794 and over £19 in 1795: not only did both he and William Toms sell corn to Job and Grigg; but William was farming a moiety of Peline – clearly in Pelynt parish, I think – before 1795 in which year a lease on lives was granted him: and he also leased part of Bury Down. I will not attempt to speculate on the relation between these two farmers and the present day families of Toms in Looe and Polperro: but once more there were farmers less than 150 years ago in a family that in later times has been chiefly on the water.

Most striking of all, however, to me was the discovery that Puckeys had been farmers; for if Puckeys can be descended from a farming family, then any fisherman in Cornwall may be – and I am left without a leg to stand on in opposition to Dr. Guppy. There seems to be evidence in Job's books of three generations of Puckey farmers. Jane Puckey bought £5 worth of lime in 1794. James bought over £10 worth in 1795, and 41lb of clover seeds in 1794: and he sold corn to Job and Grigg. I infer that James was the son of Jane; that about 1794 he was taking over the management of the farm from his mother: and that she had carried it on since her husband's death until James was old enough to relieve her: but so much is, of course, only probably inference. In 1797 a heriot was paid for Gushland on the death of James Puckey: and in May of that year Catherine Puckey paid £320 as "the consideration for adding two lives to one on Gushland": and here the inference is strong that Catherine was the widow of James. Finally in November, 1819, a second James Puckey – whom we may reasonably infer to have been the son of James and Catherine – took a new lease or grant of Gushland. If I had made these discoveries twenty-five years ago, I might perhaps have been able to identify James Puckey of Gushland and fix his position on the Puckey pedigree: but all the then oldest inhabitants of Polperro, who were my referees for family history, have – alas! – long since passed away; and the memories of the oldest living generation naturally do not go back to their great-grandfathers. Thus all my attempts to determine whether James – son of Jane and husband of Catherine – was the direct ancestor of all the Polperro Puckeys or only a collateral, have failed. What I know about the pedigree is that a Puckey – whom we will call X and who may well have been born about the same time as James – had sons William and John and James; that from William and John are descended all the Puckeys of Polperro; and that James left no descendants here. Now if one knew that X was named James, there would be a great temptation to identify him with James the elder of Gushland, and his son James with the younger James who took out the new lease in 1819: but, as I have said, no one now knows what X was named. It is remembered that his son John, as a youngster, was nicknamed "farmer"; and this lends a little – but very little – support to the suggestion that John's father was a farmer and if so identical with James of Gushland. There is, however, the obvious possibility that X was a brother or cousin of James of Gushland, and that his son earned the nickname by hanging about his kinsman's farm. Anyhow William and John, the ancestors of all the Polperro Puckeys, were obviously related to a farming family: and the significance of the name James is accentuated by the fact that a grand-daughter of X was named Catherine or Kitty – i.e. that possibly she was named after Catherine of Gushland.

It must be noted that, even at the time when one line of Puckeys was farming Gushland, other members of the family – or at least, of the same family name! – were less prosperous: for as already noted, a William Puckey was a smith, while a John Puckey – entered as "Uncle John Puckey" in 1806 – was a labourer on the land at 1s 6d per day. Whether "Uncle John Puckey" was the John born in 1760 or his father of the same name, I cannot undertake to guess: and I am bound to note the possibility that John of 1760 or his brother William of 1764 may have really been X! Nevertheless, whatever the identities may have been, the social range from farmer to labourer in the Puckeys is paralleled by a similar range in other families already noted. If we can assume that whole group of family names came into existence as the names of farmers – and this seems to me to be pretty nearly the implication from Dr. Guppy's theory – then it must be obvious that in any one family one or more branches might remain fairly prosperous, whilst others were less prosperous, and others again had definitely fallen into the ranks of day labourers: and there is therefore no cause for wonder that at the same date one Puckey was a farmer, another a smith, and another a labourer, whether or not others had already become fishermen. I have already drawn attention to the fact that two Olivers were fishermen or boatmen in 1808 – and how much earlier? – as were two of the autochthonous Libbys and a Langmaid, whilst a Philip Libby was a "tidsman" in 1781; whereas the Libbys and Langmaids are known to us as farming families. Of Cornelius Roose, who has been well in evidence in the foregoing pages, it will suffice to add that he was, no doubt, Cornelius the second, who married Ann Johns in 1769; whereas Cornelius the first, who was churchwarden of Talland in 1774, was presumably his father and identical with the Cornelius who died in 1783. Among the children of Cornelius the second were Robert and William. Robert, born 1783 or very early in 1784, married thrice: and William, born 1771, appears to be the William who in 1795 married Ann Wilcock and was the ancestor of all the Roose fishermen in Polperro. Was he the William who bought lime – though not much – in 1802 and 1803? Obviously "Cornelius Roose, junior" named in No. 44 of the

Raphiel Rental, and born in 1775-6, must have been another son. He was Cornelius the third, who in 1800 married Laetitia Houghton, to whom Cornelius the fourth was born in 1801. I suspect that Cornelius the third was tenant of Trelaske in 1816, as aforesaid.

Incidentally, as Robert's first wife was Elizabeth Houghton, it is likely enough that two brothers married two sisters.

It is also a serious question whether Barrett and Johns and Rendle on the quay-dues list of 1809 should not be included as additional examples of fishermen derived from farming families: but enough evidence has already been adduced to render unnecessary any discussion of these difficult families.

To all that I have been saying it may be retorted that a precisely reversed interpretation of the data is possible, and that the Curtis and Mark and Oliver and Puckey and Toms farmers may have been men who, or whose fathers, had risen from the ranks of fishermen. Now, of course, the data as to these families are, if taken alone, as susceptible of the one interpretation as of the other, and obviously do not demonstrate the derivation of fishermen from farmers as opposed to the reverse process. Let the conditions of the discussion, however, be borne in mind. Dr. Guppy had opined that all fishermen could be traced upwards to farmers, and had said that such derivation could definitely be shown at Salcombe: whereas I had supposed that fishing communities had been segregated for centuries from the rest of the population and had no kinship whatever with farming families. Then I discovered that in various Polperro families, now typically fishing families, there were farmers less than 150 years ago: and I have obviously to admit that this evidence tends strongly to confirm Dr. Guppy's theory and to render my own supposition baseless at any rate. Moreover in the Roose family the evidence seems to be quite definite – if the identification of William born 1771 with William married in 1796 be accepted – that all Roose fishermen of the present and several earlier generations are the lineal descendants of Cornelius the farmer: and what remains to be said strengthens the case for deriving fishermen from farmers and not vice versa.

Now, if fishermen have thus originated, what has been the process? This is a question that has required some consideration: but the analogy of modern experience seems to afford an answer. I incline to think that there was little or no direct transition in the sense of farmers' sons abandoning farming for fishing, but that they became sailors first and then, after years of ocean-going, ended their lives as fishermen, because they were unfitted for any land work, and fishing was the one available occupation. The fact that in our time at Polperro ex-Navy men and ex-merchant-seamen have ended their careers as fishermen justifies the inference that the story was the same in the past. This suggestion, however, necessarily prompts the question why farmers' sons should have abandoned farming for the sea. Now, in the first place, as English human nature is much the same during generations, we may reasonably assume that the lure of the sea was as irresistible then by some youngsters as today, and that, whether with their parents consent or in defiance of their veto, some farmers' sons abandoned the plough for the sea. Secondly, however, we must remember the activities of the Press Gang and the tremendous risks of capture that must have been run by any strapping young fellow within easy reach of a chief naval port. I suggest then that the Press Gang may have been responsible for turning many farmers' sons into sailors: and, of course, in various instances the descendants of farmers may have sunk to the status of agricultural labourers, and the sons of these may have taken to the sea or been captured by the Press Gang. I think, however, that in Polperro there was another notable factor involved: and when we come to the story of the smugglers and privateers, I shall have occasion to point out the astonishing number of farming names among them. I suggest, therefore, that the exciting and – actually or supposedly – lucrative occupations of smuggling and privateering drew away many from the farm to the sea and that, when smuggling and privateering came to an end, fishing was the one resource left to them.

*   *   *   *   *

As a pendant to this long discussion I must draw attention to the fact – attested by the sales of lime and the Eastcott rent roll – that several of the Collins or Collings family were farmers. This was a surprising discovery: for, while I can recollect only one Collings who fished, I had never supposed that any of that numerous family had been farmers. Whether these farmers were the lineal ancestors of all the families of Collings now living in the neighbourhood, or only collaterals, I cannot attempt to guess: but anyhow here again is food for thought – for the thoughtful.

In the accounts of the Records of Lansallos I noted with surprise that a Joseph Kendall was apprenticed by the parish in 1790. There are numerous references in Job's books to a Joseph Kendall, who was an agricultural labourer and was presumably uncle or cousin or father of the apprentice. Now the Kendalls had long been, and were for long afterwards, lords of the manor of Killigarth. Unless family names be an utterly delusive guide, the bonds of kinship run vertically through the social strata in sheer defiance of caste.

* * * * *

As I have already hinted, it is a matter of considerable social interest and importance to determine whether fishermen – as a crucial class-example – have been a segregated community for centuries, or whether they have been periodically recruited from the farming class. I do not propose to develop the implications here: but I will just indicate a clue. Fishermen, as a class, are and always have been relatively poor, while farmers have been – I suppose – relatively prosperous. I am afraid that what seem to be the facts about the derivation of fishermen from farmers will be more welcome to the arrant individualist than perhaps to some Socialists: and they will be very unwelcome to the out-and-out Communist, who would naturally prefer to represent any community of poorly paid workers as a segregated proletariat persisting through the centuries. However my only business is to present the facts as accurately as possible – whatever their implications.

TWO RECTORS OF LANSALLOS

There is a good deal of information about the rectory of Lansallos in Job's books: and the records not only furnish a little local history but are of considerably wider interest as affording us some insight into the manners of the times. There is no reason for assuming that the doings of two unconscionable rectors of Lansallos were abnormal or otherwise than typical of many other rectors and vicars in the West Country – and indeed in England generally. Lansallos certainly seems to have been unfortunate in its rectors: but there is good evidence for the inference that it was not peculiar in this respect. What I have to say concerns the unscrupulous absenteeism and profiteering of two successive rectors: and it may be remembered that I found at Talland episcopal licences of absenteeism made out on forms not only printed but printed expressly for the diocese of Exeter. The issue of such licences must have been on a pretty large scale to render a stock of diocesan printed forms necessary: and such evidence justifies my inference that the experiences of Lansallos were typical of those of many parishes.

In the early days of Job's books Benjamin Shipman was rector. In the table on page 57 of Couch's "History of Polperro" he is represented as succeeding Eastcott in 1785: but there is a bad blunder here. As already noted, Job's accounts with Eastcott's executors are dated 1782: but Eastcott had then been dead several years; for Shipman was already rector before the end of 1779. Whether he had been presented even earlier, and, if so, whether he had ever come into residence, I am unable to say: but at any rate in November 1779 he was entered in Job's books as "of St. Teath". Whether he had a second living in St. Teath, or why he should have lived there otherwise, I do not know: but anyhow he drew all his tithes from Lansallos and made what other profit he could out of the rectory – and remained an absentee. Of course he was bound to provide for the discharge of the statutory minimum of ecclesiastical duties; or even a bishop of those days would have been obliged to suspend or deprive him: but it was apparently easy to find some poor devil of a curate to do all the rector's work – or at any rate his statutory minimum of work – for a fraction of the pay which the rector drew for leaving it undone.

When the story opens Donnithorne was curate; and he continued in office until March, 1788. Shipman gave him £45 per year, but charged him ten guineas rent for the parsonage! Donnithorne gave up his tenancy of the house in September, 1785; but he then became tenant of the glebe, first ten guineas per year, but afterwards at £12. His curacy ended at Michaelmas, 1788: but his tenancy of the glebe continued to the following March, when Cowling – no doubt a farmer – took it over at the same rent. Donnithorne was succeeded as curate by Bedford, who was vicar of Talland: and Shipman made a good bargain by getting him at only £30 per year. How Bedford contrived to carry on the Sunday services at two churches four miles apart, or whether he limited each congregation to only morning or evening service, I do not know: bit the arrangement did not last long. Bedford's actual engagement ended apparently on 25 March, 1789: but in May he received £4 12s for taking duty on eight Sundays at 11s 6d each. Now, when he had received his first quarter's salary as curate, Job had deducted 10s, i.e. 1s 8d per day, because he had started six days after the beginning of the quarter: and since the fee of 11s 6d per Sunday is only twopence short of seven times 1s 8d, we have here a curious proof that the curate was expected to do – or was paid for doing – nothing more than Sunday duty. It may be objected that he would have to officiate occasionally at weddings and funerals: but the terms of the bishop's licence of

1816 to curate Millet – quoted in "The Records of Lansallos" – show that the curate, sometimes anyhow, took both the trifling fees for these extra jobs and the similarly trifling tithes on pigs and geese and honey.

Cory became curate at Midsummer, 1789, having previously earned £2 18s by "preaching at Lansallos church 5 Sundays". He was very nearly as cheap a bargain for the profiteering conscienceless rector as Bedford had been: for his pay was only £35 per year. His engagement legally ended suddenly on 12th January, 1790, when Shipman ceased to cumber the earth: but he was continued in his office by the succeeding rector until March, 1791.

I have a note that Shipman – in some strange fit of munificence perhaps – sent a guinea for the poor of Lansallos in April, 1780, and again in October. Job collected his tithes, paid his various outgoings, and regularly remitted the balance to him by the hand of John Oliver who duly signed an acknowledgement in Job's ledger.

The next rector was Henry Pooley, who seems to have been ready to step into Shipman's shoes at once – at any rate in so far as pay was concerned; for his share of the current half-year's tithes was reckoned from the day of Shipman's death. Since, however, he retained Cory as curate up to March, 1791, I infer that he was non-resident for his first year. He then clearly became resident for five or six years: but during 1796 or 1797 he decamped to Lostwithiel, and remained absent for the rest of his life – unless most improbably he returned for the final year or so after 1820. In 1801 he was entered in Job's ledger no longer as "of Lostwithiel" but as "of Truro"; and a record already quoted proves that in 1819 he was either living or staying temporarily at Newlyn. No doubt Lostithiel or Truro was a more pleasantly exciting residence than Lansallos, especially in winter: and no doubt it was very pleasant to draw a tithe-income for doing nothing at all, while paying some wretched curate £30 or £40 a year to do the irreducible minimum of the work that he himself had solemnly undertaken to do and was well paid for doing – if he had done it: and of course the ethics of the matter did not enter into consideration nor conscience trouble him one whit. Whether he held a second living at Lostwithiel or Truro, and so pocketed double pay, or whether he simply lived on his rectory, I do not know. Of course the conscienceless bishops of the day were as culpable as these reprobate rectors: for, while neither a bishop nor anyone else could have endowed any such a man with a sense of right and wrong, or have rendered him in the least fit to act up to his solemn but perjured professions, any bishop could have refused to grant leave of absence or to license a curate, and in that way could have compelled an incumbent to reside in his benefice – for at least one day a week. Whether such enforced residence of such rectors would have been any gain to the parishes is quite another question: and possibly Lansallos was all the sweeter for the absence of its Shipmans and Pooleys. I suppose that actually bishops and parsons alike looked on the church as a gentlemanly profession involving little to do and – in lucky cases – plenty to get, with security for life; and that the solemn promises made by each young cleric on his ordination were – as Lamb said of Coleridge's metaphysics – only his fun, and nowise to be taken seriously. Here again is abundant food for thought: but I will not discuss the matter further.

When Pooley became non-resident, he secured the services of a Kendall as curate: and I suspect that once again the curate was the vicar of Talland. We know that Charles Kendall was vicar of Talland at this time: the precedent of Bedford is suggestive: and the fact that Kendall the curate resigned his job in 1804, whilst in that same year Charles Kendall of Talland obtained episcopal leave of absence from his parish, seems to afford support to the identification. Kendall's pay as curate cannot be determined from Job's ledger-entries which repeatedly give us only "the balance of his account": but perhaps it was £45 or so.

Lake succeeded Kendall in March 1804, at £50 per year; but did not stay long. In due course he received "for serving the church from Michaelmas to Candlemas" £18 2s – a deduction of 13s for fees paid to him being made from the total of £18 15s due. In this case, therefore, the rich rector did not leave the few shillings from fees as a perquisite to the poor curate. Next a stop-gap, Pomery, got nine guineas for taking services on eight Sundays and a fast-day – the pay having gone up from 11s 6d to 21s a day in consequence, no doubt, of the increased cost of living. Millett then became curate and continued until the story ends in 1820 but presumably for the short remainder of Pooley's life beyond that date. Pooley paid him £50 a year until 1812 at least; but by 1814 the pay was raised to £65. On the other hand, however, Millett paid him, as rent for the glebe, first £13 yearly, then £15, and finally £20 by 1817. What was especially hard, however, on this poor curate was that the 10 per cent property tax, so justly levied on the rector's tithe-income, was similarly deducted from Millett's wretched pay.

On 2nd May, 1820, Job made the following entry in his last day book, No. 29:- "N.B. The Rectory sold to Rev. M. Rawlings this day for £2,800". The purchase proved a most excellent investment: for Pooley died in 1821 or so early in 1822 that that the purchaser's son became the rector in January of that year and so remained for over fifty years. In justice to Pooley I ought to add that he emulated his predecessor's munificence by giving a bushel of wheat – value 15s 6d – the poor of Lansallos in May, 1803: and I rather think that this was not his only gift of that sort.

Now let us consider the income that Shipman and Pooley drew as tithes. I have extracted and tabulated the figures for every year – except several for which the records were on pages now lost – from 1780 to 1820: but, since over a long series of years there was very little variation, the statement can be considerably condensed. I may add parenthetically that in the spring of 1781 legal proceedings were taken, evidently against tithe-payers who had failed to pay up arrears, with the result that £26 of arrears were collected in addition to £15 already paid.

The yearly – or averaged yearly – tithes were as follows:-

1780 to 1789	£186 17s 9d per year
1790 to 1796	£211 8s per year
1798 to 1800	£284 11s 11d per year
1801	£268 16s and pretty certainly arrears paid in 1801
1805	£347 12s
1806	£398 17s 9d
1807	£412 2s
1808	£423 17s
1809-11	£427 8s per year
1813	£550 19s 9d

Frank Hill Perrycoste

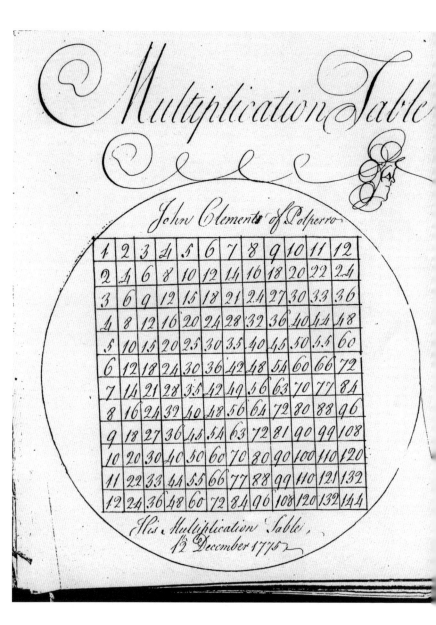

Multiplication Table

John Clements of Polperro

1	2	3	4	5	6	7	8	9	10	11	12
2	4	6	8	10	12	14	16	18	20	22	24
3	6	9	12	15	18	21	24	27	30	33	36
4	8	12	16	20	24	28	32	36	40	44	48
5	10	15	20	25	30	35	40	45	50	55	60
6	12	18	24	30	36	42	48	54	60	66	72
7	14	21	28	35	42	49	56	63	70	77	84
8	16	24	32	40	48	56	64	72	80	88	96
9	18	27	36	45	54	63	72	81	90	99	108
10	20	30	40	50	60	70	80	90	100	110	120
11	22	33	44	55	66	77	88	99	110	121	132
12	24	36	48	60	72	84	96	108	120	132	144

His Multiplication Table
12 December 1775

John Clements' Exercise Book 1775

Polperro £5 note issued by Zephaniah Job

Polperro fishermen with net cart 1907

1814   £554 11s 6d
1815   £508

After 1815 I have not the ledger figures for
gross tithes collected, but only the day-book
entries of nett balances remitted to Pooley after
payment of property tax on tithes, land tax,
poor rates, and the curate's salary less his rent
for the glebe. These nett balances for 1816, 1818
and 1819 averaged £357: and one balance in
April 1820 for the half-year was £167 6s – pretty
obviously not half of the whole year's yield. For
1815 I have both the gross amount of tithes and
the nett balance remitted: and since the former
was £508, and the latter £356, we may reckon that
Pooley got a little more than £500 a year up to
1819 or 1820. Now the tremendous increase in
the tithe income – which in 1814 was very nearly
treble that of the yearly income from 1780-1789
– resulted, of course, from the extravagantly high
price of corn: so that, while the poor starved,
absentee incumbents, who did nothing to earn
even their normal income, grew richer and richer
on this doubly unearned increment. The income
for the first decade under notice should have been
a moderately comfortable one if we consider the
level of prices at that date: but later this income
was practically trebled; whereas it will be found,
when we come to the section on prices, that these
were far from being trebled.

In addition to pocketing the farmers' tithes
the rectors took good care to collect their tithes
from the fishermen. In very many cases these
are expressly entered as sean – properly scean
– tithes: and we hear of "the Gannet sean" and
"the old sean": but in other cases they are simply
entered as the fishermen's tithes. Unquestionably
the scean fishery afforded the greater part of the

tithes: but I hesitate to infer that this alone was tithed, and that "sean" was merely omitted in some entries. My reasons are (1) that the entries sometimes seem rather to imply that the tithes were of both sceaned fish and other fish, and (2) that the payments to the crier – already quoted – to warn the men, would hardly have been necessary if only the – probably well-known – owners of scean nets were liable. However I do not feel confident about this matter.

The figures indicate so much variation in the yield of the fishery, and the notes are in some cases so interesting, that it may be worth while to tabulate the tithes year by year – especially as an average would be fairly meaningless when the range was so great. Here then are the figures and notes.

	£	s	d	
1780	7	10	10	
1781	11	1	4	
1782	7	18	2	
1783	7	14	6	
1784	6	11	6	
1785	3	16	0	
1786	3	10		
1787	5	4	4	"a moiety" for 2 years noted against ½-year in April.
1788	4	13	8	"moiety sean fish tithe" in April half year.
1789	5	15	3	
1790	4	13	6½	
1791	9	16	4	"moiety of Polperro sean fish tithe" against £9-9-10 in April.
1792	8	18	3	
1793	16	7	3	"sean fish tithe" against 14/4/9 in April.
1794	6	8	5	"for lodging two seans."

1795	12	3	4
1796	13	10	2	includes three halves in April – one for another year.
1797	2	1	0
1798		19	6	"Mr Kendall received the other half."
1799	1	12	6
1800	5	10	8	proportion of sean fish tithe in April: "fishermen's tithe received per list"" in October.
1801	4	19	3
1802	missing		
1803	(2	1	11)	first half year's entries missing
1804	(1	15	7)	first half year's entries missing
1805	11	12	7
1806	16	17	7	sean 15-10-0: "fishermen's tithe" 1-7-0.
1807	20	1	0
1808	1	9	3	October payment only.
1809	1	11	0
1810	1	19	0	"per list"
1811	1	19	0
1812	-	-	-
1813	2	0	3
1814	-	-	-
1815	1	15	4	from sean.

The sudden falling off in 1797, and the low yield during several successive years, are so remarkable that I surmised, in explanation thereof, that nearly all the fishermen were too busily engaged in smuggling to attend to fishing. This explanation, however, will not account for the trifling yield from 1808 to 1815, because – as will be shown in due course – I can find no evidence of smuggling during this period. Possibly the Navy and the privateers had drained off most of the fishermen then.

It will be noticed that in various years the Rector of Lansallos received only a moiety or a half of the scean tithes: and I had to consider what might be the explanation. I think that we may safely infer that on some occasions the scean had been drawn partly in Lansallos and partly in Talland or Lanteglos – if the parishes be assumed to include the sea adjacent! – or possibly that the fishermen were half of them living on the Lansallos side of Polperro and half of them on the Talland side. The note in 1798 that "Mr Kendall received the other half" would be conclusive evidence for this interpretation had not Kendall also been curate at Lansallos in 1798. However, it seems most highly improbable that Pooley allowed his curate, as such, to take half the fish-tithes; and, if he had, then there should have been only moieties for himself during the whole period 1797 to 1820: so I think we may accept the bi-parochial interpretation.

In conclusion I must add that it would be difficult to find more revolting examples of ecclesiastical greed than those afforded by the heartless plunder of poor fishermen and cottagers by tithing fish and pigs and geese and honey. Although, of course, I utterly disapprove of the allocation of farmers' tithes to the Church, I necessarily recognise that the tenant farmer is none the worse off for paying them, because, if tithes were abolished, the rent would be exactly so much increased: while the landowner has bought or inherited his land as tithable land. The case of the fishermen and cottagers is, however, utterly different: and the parsons who tithed them were extorting legalised plunder. One bitterly regrets that the Polperro fishermen could not have treated Shipman and Pooley as the parson in the song was treated who demurred to the size of his tithe pig. They should have told the absentee rector to collect his tithe himself from the scean, and deal with his prey as best he could.

I can now more than justify the statement made in an earlier section that, if Pooley had contributed to the help of the starving fishermen in 1817 only what he had taken from them in tithes, his subscription would have thrown Lord Granville's into the shade: for it appears that up to 1815 he had received nearly £150 of this ill-gotten gain.

THE TRAFFIC IN CHURCHES

This section will form a sort of pendant to the foregoing in so far as concerns what I have here called the traffic in churches: and some of the story is very astonishing even after one has realised the state of affairs at Lansallos. Let us consider the doings of Sir Harry Trelawny, who was himself in ecclesiastical orders. He somehow had possession of the living of St. Allen, which, I believe, is near Truro: and it would seem that he either took up residence there for a time, or anyhow was staying there, and that Lady Trelawny was there in August, 1791. Moreover Job paid a curious bill for crockery and glass and knives and forks, etc., supplied to St. Allen's: and I must say that this expenditure was on the simplest and most economical scale. Perhaps the intention was to buy simply what was really necessary for a poor curate – and meanwhile Sir Harry put up with these makeshifts during perhaps a brief sojourn there. Whether he somehow managed to take services there at intervals during the two years, or whether he got someone to deputise for him I cannot say: but it is notable that there is nothing whatever in the accounts about any pay to a curate; while the tithes were so low that there would not have been very much left after paying a curate – even on the normal scale – and meeting other expenses. I have the following record of tithes.

October 1791 - £37 6s 7d
April 1792 - £34 7s 7d
November 1792 - £34 17s 2d
April 1793 - £35 9s 5d

In addition there was in April, 1792, a half-year's rent of the glebe, and in April, 1793, a year's rent - £17 5s and £34 respectively.

As against these takings there were expenses in

October, 1791, of £15 0s 6d,
November, 1792, of £4 16s
April, 1793, of £45 3s 10d.

As this last account of expenses included £5 4s 9d for fish, whilst in 1792 there were bills of £1 13s 4d for beer and £2 3s 8d for coals, it looks as though Sir Harry spent some time at St. Allen's. The figures show that in twenty-four months the nett proceeds were £128 6s 8d; though, if the glebe had been let for the whole time instead of only for eighteen months, the nett total would have been just over £146, i.e. £73 per year. In 1793 and 1794 the Rev. Nicholas Dyer "of Venn, in Devon" seems to have held St. Allen's and to have paid Gilbert in 1793 and Bluett in 1794 to do the work – giving Bluett at any rate £35 per year. Thereafter St. Allen's passes from our ken. One infers that Sir Harry sold or assigned the living to Dyer: but evidently there is behind these accounts a good deal of history to which we have not much clue. However, Nicholas Dyer can be added to the list of profiteering absentee parsons.

* * * * *

The living of Egloshayle, near Wadebridge, was in Sir Harry's hands for nearly a dozen years: and here again we cannot extract a full history from Job's accounts. It seems clear that either an actual curate or some deputy was paid to take the services: for in 1798 the glebe and garden were let to an ecclesiastic; and in 1799 e.g. Sir Harry paid one "for serving" at Egloshayle. In the years 1793 to 1797 the tithes seem to have been between £160 and £180 per year – with £33 extra in 1795 on Sir William Molesworth's woods in Egloshayle, which evidently were then felled: but in 1798 they seem to have passed £200 in addition to £20 rent for the glebe and £2 2s for the garden. The tithes were £220 in 1802, nearly £209 in 1803 plus £18 18s on coppice, and £104 in the earlier half of 1804. In this last year some arrangement was made with Cory of St. Keynes – perhaps our old acquaintance of Lansallos – by which he received £26 16s 3d as his "proportion" of the tithes from 7th June to Michaelmas: but as Cory got only £9 7s 1d out of the tithes in 1805, one is puzzled to know what the arrangement was and whether here again barefaced trafficking was going on.

The expenses at Egloshayle were heavy – over £25 for the second half of 1793, £37 in 1794, nearly £120 in 1795, over £95 in 1796, over £90 in 1797 and £135 13s 6d in 1798 when "sundry bills paid at Egloshayle" amounted to £104. One item of this year was a bill for wages etc., due to Rebecca Warne – probably for several years – amounting to £19 14s. In 1802 the expenses were over £165, in 1803 over £77 and 1804 over £158, i.e. very nearly as much as Sir Harry himself got in tithes. I feel unable to say whether these expenses did or did not include the pay of a curate or deputy: and the whole story is rather a puzzle which possibly some letters buried in the twenty-five pounds weight of Job's correspondence may one day clear up.

In addition to the tithes proper at Egloshayle there were in several years those detestable tithes on pigs and geese and – in one year – honey also. These yielded 10s 6d in 1796, £3 1s in 1797, and 12s 6d in the earlier half of 1798.

In simple justice to Sir Harry it must be said that he did more for Egloshayle in eleven years than Pooley did for Lansallos in thirty. He seems to have taken some personal interest in the place and visited it or stayed there at times. He paid for the schooling of some children: and the expenses of 1795 included a lot for schooling. The expenses for 1796 seem to have included some charities: and in 1798 he subscribed £11 to "the voluntary contribution for Egloshayle parish".

* * * * *

So far we have been concerned with the doings of churchmen: but the most remarkable thing of all about this eighteenth century traffic in churches is that our old acquaintance Thomas Eastcott of Port Looe, a layman and aged 25 in 1795, was at that date in possession of the rectory of St. Stephen's at Saltash, and was augmenting his income very appreciably by the tithes that he drew from that parish. For this rectory he paid a conventionary rent of £266 per year to the Dean and Canons of Windsor: and late in 1796 he paid them £1,207 3s 4d for a renewal of his holding. In 1797 he mortgaged the rectory for £1,000: and unless "the rectory" meant simply the parsonage house – which I very much doubt – the security for the mortgage was uncommonly good, as the tithes were £601 in

1796, £566 in 1797, and £619 in 1798. Thus after deducting the conventionary rent he drew from the tithes an average income of £330 less interest and sinking fund on the price for renewal. He worked the living by paying a curate £40 per year. In 1799 the parishioners perhaps rebelled against this whole scandalous state of affairs: for in April Job debited Eastcott £5 15s 5d "to Expce at St. Stephens when the Parishioners refused to raise the composition for tithes".

How Eastcott came into possession of the rectory, and whether he inherited it from his father, I cannot say. I found no entry of tithes credited to him before 1795; and I found nothing about the rectory in the accounts of his mother or with her executors during his minority: whereas, if the rectory had been in the hands of his father there would surely have been relevant credits to Mrs Eastcott and her executors. On the other hand, after several years the rectory disappears from Thomas Eastcott's accounts. Thus the whole business is a puzzle.

It seems clear that Eastcott was not what is called a "lay rector", i.e. one who holds rectorial or greater tithes which before the Reformation had in so many cases enriched the monks, and on the dissolution of the monasteries were scandalously misbestowed on courtiers and others and have been bought and sold many times. The "lay rector" neither holds the church-living nor – as such - is the owner of the advowson, but simply has a lien on the rectorial tithes. Eastcott was apparently rector in some ecclesiastical sort of sense, since he paid a curate to do the work which, as a layman, he could not do if he had – most improbably – wished to do it. Then there is the curious business of the rent and fine for renewal paid to the dean and canons of Windsor: and it is a striking commentary on the ecclesiastical morals – or lack of morals – at this period that these fashionable and highly respectable churchmen lined their pockets by this disgraceful traffic.

As I have said, the whole story is a great puzzle: but I have given the facts – and possibly some one else can explain them and can adduce parallel examples.

PRICES OF COMMODITIES

The data for this section constitute a sheer embarrassment of riches: and it is very possible that it would be well worth the while of a student of prices to work laboriously through Nos. 2 and 3 – and perhaps some of the daybooks and ledgers also! – in order to extract far fuller and more details lists than those subjoined.

First of all I tabulate the prices of grain over a long series of years, giving the respectively lowest and highest prices that I have noted in each year. If the complete series of grain trade books from 1786 to 1820 had been extant, it would have been more satisfactory, for two reasons, to rely solely upon these, and to ignore all the other records of the prices of grain scattered through the day-books. In the first place I could then have tabulated by harvests instead of by the civil years, tracing the rise and fall from September to the spring, and bringing out the interesting fact, which I noticed, that occasionally there was a marked rise or fall of price in the late spring conditioned, obviously, by the forecast of a bad or good coming harvest. Secondly the prices would then have all have been wholesale – i.e. as paid by Job and Grigg to the farmers: whereas actually in my tables these prices are mixed with retail prices of single bushels. However, as the difference between wholesale and retail price must often have been no more than – and sometimes less than – the variation of wholesale prices during the year, this lack of homogeneity in the data is not serious. Eventually I regretted having extracted any corn prices from Nos. 7 and 8: for it seemed to me that sometimes Job and Grigg had sold corn at a lower price than they paid for it at about the same date! I could only surmise that they had made sale contracts forward in the expectation of a good harvest and cheap corn, and had been unfortunate in their forecast. Several extra low prices from these sales-books I decided to omit as – on this supposition – misleading.

Finally, in studying these prices of corn, we have to remember that the Cornish bushel was apparently twice as much as the statutory bushel. Since the publication of the earlier sections of these records I have received some further information about Cornish measures from Mr Lewis Julian, who says that even in his younger days corn was sold either by the "Short Bushel" of 4 pecks, or by the "Long Bushel" of 6 pecks, and that these Cornish pecks contained 4 gallons instead of two. Thus, whereas the statutory bushel contains 8 gallons, the "Short" has 16 and the "Long" 24! We have to conclude that Job and his neighbours bought and sold corn by the "Short" bushel exactly twice the standard capacity: and I suppose that their "pecks" and "bushels" of potatoes were also twice the respective standards. Had I not looked into Nos. 7 and 8, I should have supposed the "bushel" to be really a bushel; whereas actually it was equal to two statutory bushels, so that prices per "bushel" must be understood as prices of two bushels.

PRICES PER BUSHEL

	Barley		Oats		Wheat	
1780	-	4/-	12/-	-	-	-
1781	-	-	-	-	13/-	-
1782	-	5/-	-	-	-	-
1784	-	-	6/-	5/6	-	-
1785	6/6	3/-	4/9	7/-	-	-
1786	6/6	5/-	6/6	3/6	9/-	10/-
1787	5/-	5/3	3/3	5/-	9/-	10/6
1788	5/-	5/6	3/3	5/-	12/-	10/-
1789	5/-	6/6	3/6	4/9	10/-	14/-
1790	6/3	7/-	3/6	5/-	12/6	13/10
1791	7/-	5/6	3/9	5/6	9/-	10/6
1792	4/6	5/9	5/3	5/-	10/6	8/6
1793	6/-	6/6	6/-	7/3	-	-
1794	9/-	6/9	7/6	6/-	11/-	12/3
1795	8/-	7/-	9/-	7/-	15/-	20/-
1796	7/-	9/-	-	-	21/-	18/-
1797	7/-	-	6/-	-	-	-
1798	7/-	-	5/-	5/6	20/-	16/-
1799	-	-	6/-	-	-	-
1800	-	-	11/-	13/-	-	-
1801	-	-	-	-	-	-
1802	8/6	10/-	5/6	7/6	-	-
1803	5/-	6/6	6/-	9/-	15/-	15/6
1804	5/6	6/-	6/-	7/6	-	-
1805	-	-	6/3	6/9	-	-
1806	8/9	-	-	-	-	-
1807	9/2	10/-	9/6	6/6	21/-	-
1808	8/6	10/6	10/-	12/-	18/6	24/-
1809	9/-	11/-	9/-	10/6	21/-	26/-
1810	9/-	12/-	9/-	6/-	21/-	28/-
1811	-	-	-	-	-	-
1812	21/-	14/-	-	-	26/-	31/-
1813	17/-	9/6	-	-	30/-	24/-
1814	10/-	6/6	7/6	8/-	20/-	-
1815	5/6	6/6	6/6	10/-	20/-	14/-
1816	5/-	11/-	6/6	8/-	16/-	32/-
1817	16/-	10/-	7/6	-	30/-	25/-
1818	10/-	15/-	8/6	11/6	22/-	17/6
1819	14/-	7/-	10/6	9/-	19/-	15/-
1820	5/-	8/6	-	-	16/-	19/-
1821	5/-	5/6	-	-	-	-

Presumably any experienced farmer can draw from the foregoing tables inferences as to the weather and the harvests in various years: but there were other factors besides, especially in the case of wheat prices. In 1797 the bank of England ceased to pay gold – the country being then in the throes of a great war – and the purchasing power of bank notes began to fall below their face value. From our own recent experience we know all about this sort of disturbance in prices: but the question at once arises whether the foregoing prices after 1797 were reckoned in bank paper or in bullion. In either case the price of barley in 1812 was extraordinary, since it then was at 21s for a time: and it was as high as 17s during part of 1813: whereas it had been as low as 5s in 1803, and was down to that level early in 1816 and in 1820 and 1821. The price of 3s during part of 1795 was a record apparently. The most striking entry about oats is that of 1780 when the price was 12s; for it was not until 1800 that this price was again reached. It is unfortunate that I have no prices of wheat in 1780: but, as barley was cheap, the harvest cannot have been a general failure.

The prices of wheat were partly conditioned by the artificial factor of the corn laws as well as by the suspension of payment in gold in 1797: but several harvests in the last decade of the century, especially those of 1795 and 1797, were so deficient that bounties were paid on the import of corn. The wheat prices from 1807 onwards are instructive, and fully explain that great increase in the value of tithes as already noted and the great increase of rents which will be noted later.

I subjoin a table of the prices of clover seeds. The curious feature is that, whereas the price of clover was no higher in 1820 than in 1786, that of Dutch clover had more than doubled during this period. The prices of all three seeds were remarkably low in 1816.

PRICES PER POUND

	Clover		Dutch Clover	Trefoil	
1786	1/-	1/2	-/7	-	
1787	1/1	1/3	-/8	-	
1788	-/8	-/11	-	-/6½	-/7
1789	-/8	-	-	-/4	-/4½
1793 or 94 or 95	-	-/9½	-	-/5	
1803	1/-	1/2	-	-/8	
1804	-/11	1/8	-	-/8	
1807	1/-	-	1/3	-/6	
1808	1/-	-	1/1	-	
1809	1/4	-	1/5	-/8	
1810	1/4	1/6	1/6	-/8	
1815	-/11	-	-	-	
1816	-/8	-	1/-	-/4	
1817	1/4	-	1/6	-/9	
1818	1/-	-	-	-	
1819	1/2	-	1/6	-/8	
1820	1/-	-	-	-	

* * * * *

Next let us take the prices of various articles of food, beginning with the products of the farm, and remembering that a Cornish "bushel" of potatoes was apparently two standard bushels. Very little comment seems to be required on these prices: for the steady rise in those of meat and cheese tells its own story. The price of butter, at any rate after 1781, seems to have been very high relatively to other prices. It is curious that eggs were practically 8d per dozen in March, 1794, against 5d in October 1792: and it is very annoying that, although Wills bought so many eggs at Trelawne, he hardly every entered the number bought for his outlay. The prices of 2½d per pound in 1781, and 2¼d in 1789 for beef – of sorts – agree fairly well with the Talland Records of 2d per pound in 1751 and 1759: but after 1791 prices seem to have risen steadily.

I was very much astonished by the relatively tremendous price of ling, which even now can be bought in Polperro at 4d per lb, and could be got at 2d thirty years ago. I concluded that the ling in question was not only salted – as packets of over 100 pounds were sent to Sir Harry Trelawny in London – but probably boned also: and, on inquiry, I learned from one of our fishermen that in the old days ling was salted and prepared with very great care here, so that it apparently must have been rather a delicacy. These prices therefore were clearly not those of fresh ling: but, on the other hand the low price of salmon is very remarkable. It will be noted that tea was very much dearer than now, and sugar three times as dear, whereas the prices of coffee and chocolate were not very different from those of the present day. I do not know that any further remarks on the following tables are needed.

POTATOES per bushel. - 1780, March, 5/6. 1781, January, 6/-. 1781, February, 5/3. 1796, January, March and October, 5/-. 1797, June, 4/-. 1807, April, 4/-. 1810, July, 8/-. 1818, June, 5/-. (10/- per peck in 1793 is obviously an error – probably for 10d, which would equal ¾ per bushel).

BUTTER per pound. - 1781, May, 5¾d. 1789, January, 7d and 7½. 1789, January, 8d. November, 1792 to September 1795, 9d and 1lb at 10d. 1795, 9d, 8d, 10d, 10½d. 1796, March, 1/-, April, 9½d, October, 9½d.

CHEESE per pound. - 1787, 5d. 1795, 4d. 1796, 6½d. 1798, 7d. 1810 (Cheshire) 1/-. 1811 (ditto ? ?) 1/-.

EGGS. - 1792, October, 1/3 for 35. 1794, March, 10/- for 184.

HONEY. - 1788, 10d per pint.

BEEF, per pound. - 1781, shoulder, 2½d (for

a 22lb joint). 1789, 3d, 3½d, 3¾d. 1789, neck, 2¼d. 1791, 3d, 3½d. 1794, 4d. 1795, sirloin, 5d. 1795, rump, 5d. 1796, 5d. 1815, leg, 6d, sirloin, 6½d, "rost piece" 7d (all huge joints in 1815). 1817, 6d. 1818, 8d.

MUTTON, per pound. – 1791, 3½d, 4½d. 1791, lamb, 2½d. 1794, mutton, 3¼d, 4d. 1795, mutton, 5½d. 1796, mutton, 3¾d, 4½d. 1800, legs of mutton, 3/6 each. 1817, mutton, 6d per lb.

TALLOW, per pound. – 1789, 4d, 4½d. 1791, 4d. 1794, beef tallow, 6d. 1795, beef tallow, 8d. 1795, mutton tallow, 7½d.

PORK, per pound. – 1781, 3d, 4d. 1782, 3½d. 1803, 5d. 1804, 5½d.

FOWLS (and CHICKENS) each. – 1779, November, 10d. 1780, October, 9d. 1791, 6d, 6½d. 1792 (chickens) 3½d. 1792, fowls, 6½d, 7d, 9d. 1794, fowls, 10d, 7d, 6d. 1794 (chickens), 5d, 7d. 1795 (small chickens), 6 for 1/1. 1796, fowls, 1/2. 1804, fowls, 1/6. 1816, fowls, 8d.

DUCKS, each – 1781, about 6d. 1788, 10d. 1791, 1/-. 1792, 9d, 11d. 1792 (young), 9½d. 1793, 1/-. 1794, 1/-, 1/3. 1802, 1/6. 1806, 1/2.

GEESE. – 1792, fat goose, 4d per lb. 1810, 4/2 and 4/8 each. 1810, giblets, 1/6. 1817, goose, 3/6. 1818, goose, 4/4.

TURKEYS. – 1779, 6/-. 1804, £1 0s 10d for 3. 1808, 5/-.

WILD DUCK. – 1789, 7½d.

HARE. – 1795, 1/-.

LING, per pound. – 1793, February, 2½d and 1794, April, 3d, in over 100lb parcels. 1800,, February, March, 5d. 1800, April, 2d.

TURBOT. – 1800, 5d per lb.

SALMON. – 1795, 3d per lb.

SALMON PEEL. – 1803, 6d per lb.

CRABS and LOBSTERS. – 1791, crab. 3d. 1795, crab, 6d. 1794, lobster, 6d. 1799, 2 crabs and 4 lobsters, 4/6.

TEA, per pound. – 1794, Souchong, 4/-. 1795, "Tea" 5/- and 7/-. 1795, Hyson, 5/6 (ex Guernsey?). 1796, Souchong, 6/-. 1796, Hyson, 7/-. 1796, Pekoe, 9/-. 1797, Souchong, 5/-. 1798 "Tea" 5/- (smuggled?). 1816, ditto, 7/6. 1817, ditto, 7/-. 1819, ditto, 7/-.

COFFEE and CHOCOLATE, per pound. – 1794, coffee, 1/1. 1797, "best grey coffee" 2/- . 1817, chocolate, 2/6 and 2/9. 1818, chocolate, 2/6 and 2/9.

LEMONS. – 1794, 2½d each.

"SUGGAR" – 1796, 9d per lb.

"FRAIL FIGS" – 1795, £1 9s 8d.

STRASBURG SNUFF, from Guernsey, 1/- per lb in 1794.

VINEGAR. – 1792, 4d per quart.

There are various entries of the cost of wine and spirits: but, as these were so frequently obtained from the smugglers presumably – in some cases avowedly so – we cannot assume that the Polperro prices were the same as those current in the country generally. The prices of cider and beer, however, are in a different category: and we may take these first.

Cyder:- 1786, £1 19s per cask. "Paid Mr William Hardin for a Hogshead Cyder (very good). 70 gallons £1 1s." (The comment "very good" was added – evidently after trial – in different ink).

1794	£1 17 0	per hogshead
1795	£1 7 0	„ „
1797	£2 5 0	„ „
1799	£3 3 0	„ „
1809	£3 10 0	„ „
1818	£3 12 6	„ „
1818	£3 17 6	„ „

The rise in the price of cyder is very remarkable:

and I do not in the least understand it: but perhaps some farmer can suggest an explanation. It is a nuisance that we do not know whether the "cask" of 1786 was a hogshead or of a larger capacity: but, if it was a hogshead, I think that Job must have got his "very good" cyder of the next entry from Harding at half the market price – in which case he was ungrateful in mutilating Harding's name.

Next let us take the prices of beer.
1798 Beer   £1   6 8 per barrel
1798   Porter £1 16 0 ,,   ,,
1803 ,,   £1 11 6 ,, cask
1804 ,,   £2   4 0 ,, barrel
1805 ,,   £2   6 0 ,,   ,,
1810 ,,   £2 12 6 ,,   ,,
1805 Stout   £3   1 6 ,,   ,,
1808 Whitbreads £2 6 0   ,,

The rise in the price of porter, though far less than that of cyder, is again notable: but why was Whitbread's Stout so much cheaper than the other, unless – as I suspect – it was really porter.

In dealing with the prices of wines and spirits we are faced by the difficulty that these are so often quoted per anker. This was quite a new unit of capacity to me: but, on consulting a dictionary of 1805, I found that the anker – Dutch ancker – contains "about eight gallons". Unfortunately, however, in one of the subjoined entries we are told that the anker contained 10 gallons, and in another $7\frac{1}{4}$: and I have noticed "a large anker", specified in Job's books. It is therefore hazardous to calculate the price per gallon from that per anker when we have no other data: and, though in several instances another entry suggests a clue, I have added the price per gallon only interrogatively where there is any uncertainty.

BRANDY

1787   4/6 per gallon.

1792   4/6 per gallon.

1793   3/6 per gallon (direct from smugglers?).

1795   Barely 3/- per gallon (ie. 3.6 for 9½ pints, sent to Trelawne "by the Shepherd").

1796   5/4 per gallon, including cost of cask (ie. £1 12 for a six gallon cask supplied to Eastcott by smugglers).

1797   6/2 per gallon including cost of six gallon cask.

1797   9/- per gallon.

1799   £2 10s per anker.

1801   £1 14s per anker "sent me from Guernsey".

Here again there was a notable advance in price, unless in the later years a far better brandy was supplied. If the anker of 1799 held eight gallons, the price at 6/3 per gallon would accord with one price of 1797: while Job in 1801 can hardly have paid more than 4/3 per gallon for his private supply. It may be remembered that there is a Talland record of brandy at 1/- per quart, ie. 4/- per gallon retail, in 1736.

Now let us take the prices of gin and rum.

1793   Gin 11/- per anker (direct to Job from Guernsey).

1795   Gin 7/6 per gallon (including cost of cask).

1798   Gin £2 6s per anker (ie. 7/6 per gallon?).

1798   Rum £3 3s per anker (ie. 9/- per gallon?).

1800   Rum 9/8 per gallon (anker of 7¼ gallons).

Finally there are the prices of wine as below:-

1784   "Wine" 5/6 per gallon.

1796   Port 6/9½ per gallon (ie. £3 8s for anker of 10 gallons supplied to Sir Harry Trelawny by the smugglers).

1798   Port £1 18s per anker.

1798   Port £2 5s per anker.

1798   Port £2 13s per anker, "first cost and freight only". (Supplied, no doubt, by the smugglers, to Sir Harry).

1799   Port £2 per anker (from Guernsey).

1799   Port £2 4s per anker; £2 6s; £2 8s; all from Guernsey?

1800   Port £2 per anker, from Guernsey.

1819   Port £58 per pipe of 138 gallons at Oporto. The duty paid was £52 6s 6d at 7/7 per gallon; and the freight, etc. etc, accounted for £4 9s 6d. Thus altogether the wine cost Sir Harry Trelawny 16/7½ per gallon: and he must have recalled with a sigh of regret those past times when the Polperro smugglers supplied his port wine at 6/9, or even less, per gallon.

There remain only three wine records:-

1799   Sherry £1 for 12 bottles – bottles included (equivalent to 1/6 per quart (?) at most).

1799 and 1800. Sherry £2 10s for a large anker (probably 5/- per gallon) with cask included.

1798. Claret £4 3s for box of 30 bottles – box included (ie. under 2/6 per quart – if quart bottles were supplied – for the actual wine; since we know from the Talland Records that at this date quart bottles cost 3½ each)   .

*   *   *   *   *

Next after the prices of food and drink let us take those of coal as tabulated opposite.

Coals, per quarter equals 12 cwt.

1791 April, 12/-
1793 Spring, 12/- ex vessel
1793 April, 16/6 ex vessel
1793 September, 14/-
1794 February, 16/-
1794 March, 12/6 ex vessel
1795 August 14/-
1796 July, 14/6
1796 September, 16/- ex cellar
1798 March, 15/6 ex vessel (?)
1798 December, 15/-
1799 November, 18/- ex vessel apparently
1802 14/-
1803 March, 21/-
1803 April, 17/-
1803 December, 20/- and 21/-
1804 December, 18/-
1807 April, 21/-
1808 April, 23/- ex cellar
1808 Later in year, 21/- ex vessel
1809 October, 22/- ex vessel
1810 March, 24/- ex vessel
1810 May, 24/-
1810 November, 23/-
1815 April, 19/-
1815 September, 17/- ex vessel
1816 August, 13/6
1818 September, 15/-
1819 August, 14/- (costing Job 13/3?)

The rise from 12/- per quarter in 1791 to 18/- in 1799; the sudden drop to 14/- in 1802, followed by the rise to 21/- in 1803; the price of 24/- in 1810; the fall to 19/- and 17/- in 1815, and to 13/6 in 1816 – ie. almost to the level of twenty-five years earlier – were nowise erratic changes, but become perfectly intelligible if a chronological table of wars be consulted. The price rose during the earlier war with France, fell sharply on the conclusion of the Peace of Amiens in 1802, went up 50 per cent when war broke out again in 1803 – in fact a month ahead of the renewal – had fallen considerably after Napoleon's deportation to Elba, and went down and down after Waterloo. What proportion of the increased price during war was merely coal's share in the general increase brought about by war, I cannot say: but I think it certain that much was due to the dangers, and consequently increased expense, of transport by sea. I happened to light on a letter in which Job apologised to his correspondent for failing to send a cargo of grain, for a coasting vessel had refused to take it on account of the risk of capture by French privateers. I conclude, therefore, that these enemy craft played a large part in putting up the cost of coals and all other seaborne goods.

There are some rather puzzling accounts of payments for candles used at Trelawne which afford us some clue – unhappily not very precise – as to the expense of lighting a fairly large house at this period. First of all, here are the actual data.

> January, 1794 - £8 4s for candles.
> February, 1798 - £28 18s 6d for candles.
> May, 1799 - £27 11s 4d for candles and soap.
> December, 1800 - £15 10s 8d for candles.

I could find no account for candles in 1795, 1796, 1797 in the ledger: so, unless they were covered by some cash payment in those years, one might assume that the 1798 payment covered four years. Against accepting this interpretation there is the awkward obstacle of practically the same payment in 1799 for twelve or sixteen months, although this covered soap also. I incline to think that they yearly expense of lighting varied from £8 to £27 accordingly as the family spent months away from Trelawne or the whole year there: but in some early years of the nineteenth century there are the following accounts.

August, 1804 - £11 12s for candles.
August, 1805 - £3 6s 9d for candles and soap.
October, 1807 - £4 16s (or ? £6 16s) for candles.

THE COST OF LIVING

Given all the fore-going data as to the prices of food and fuel – and the prices of candles as previously quoted in "The Records of Talland" – what was the cost of living apart from the cost of clothes? A few stray records indicate that for simple living the cost – in Cornwall at any rate – was not only considerably lower of course than at present, but also considerably lower than in the first decade of this century. Thus from 1790 to 1793 the Eastcott girls – daughters of the former rector of Lansallos – boarded with a Mrs Williams while they were at school, and paid her £7 10s each for six months' board. If this charge really covered twenty-six weeks, it works out at 5s 9¼d per week: and, after deducting from this Mrs Williams' dues for laundry and service and house-room, we get a pretty low price for food even if she charged the girls only cost price thereof. At an appreciably later date, namely about 1808, the account of Miss Quiller – beneficiary under her father's will – was debited £7 7s for half a year's board with her mother. This works out at 5s 7¾d per week – presumably for food alone: and, as the cost of various articles of food had increased since 1790, the agreement with the charge to the Eastcott girls is fairly close. In June 1798 Job paid two guineas for four weeks' "lodging" for

Captain Eastcott's wife: but unluckily one cannot determine whether she was charged half a guinea per week for –probably relatively expensive – lodging alone, or whether board was included. In 1808, £1 weekly was paid for "Mr Trelawny"; and I presume that this covered both lodging and board beyond mere simple sufficiency, and possibly included wine or beer: but unfortunately again our data are insufficient.

There are two hotel bills exhibiting very different charges. On a loose slip of paper dated 7th March, 1798, someone – I should think very likely a clerk or employee of Job's – accounted for his expenses on a journey: and we learn that his breakfast cost him sixpence ands his dinner a shilling. This was cheap enough: but, when Job and Mrs Braddon made a journey to Launceston in 1812, dinner – for only two presumably – cost 17s 6d, and tea for three 4s 6d. I think that wine must have accounted for a very large part of the dinner bill: and tea at 1s 6d per head must have been very "high" tea. I shall return to these hotel bills when dealing with the cost of travelling.

There is a series of entries of expenses incurred by Lansallos Parish for the maintenance in Exeter Asylum of poor James Henna – obviously the former tenant on the Manor of Raphiel. The parish paid £16 10s in May 1805: and this payment presumably covered twenty-two weeks, as we are told definitely that the charge from Michaelmas 1806 to Easter 1807 was at 15s per week – besides a guinea as "extra fee to doctor". In January 1810 eighteen weeks "board" etc, cost £12 – ie. 13s 4d per week; in May there was a payment of £12 15s for the amount to 24 April, and in September £15 2s 5d – apparently at 15s per week from Christmas in the former case, while the September bill must surely have included special charges besides maintenance. In December 1812 Job receives £24 1s 8d for expenses re Henna; and in November 1817 "for James Henna's maintenance at Exeter Asylum to 30th September 1817 by order and for account of Rev. T. (?) Howell" £20 5s. In neither case do we know what period was covered by the payment: but there is the certain fact that Henna cost as much as 15s per week, and as little as 13s 4d in 1809, for maintenance in a public asylum.

I thought it desirable to quote these few data as to the cost of living in immediate sequence to the tables or prices of food and fuel: but there are yet other prices to be considered – chiefly those of animals for which the data are numerous.

PRICES OF COWS.

1792	£7 10s
1793	£7 15s (a Guernsey)
1796	£12 12s
1797	£12
1797	£12 14s (at Liskeard fair)
1798	£45 0s 6d for 3 fat cows (weighing) 14 unintelligible units at £2 15s per unit)
1798	£40 10s for 3 fat cows
1799	£11 (a Jersey)
1799	£12 (each Jersey)
1799	£12 15s (at Liskeard fair)
1799	£13 2s 6d (at Liskeard fair)
1799	£14 4s 4d ("a cow killed – after having calved": sold off the Trelawne estate)
1803	£9 7s 6d (each for Jerseys)
1803	£9 9s and £11 11s and apparently £10
1804	£6 6s and £9 10s and £13 12s
1804	£12 12s and £14
1806	£15 (Jersey)
1807	£12
1808	£16 10s

1809	£15
1810	£12 and £20
1814	£10
1815	£10
1816	£15 8s 9d (a fat cow)
1819	£14 15s and £10 10s and £10 and £9 10s and 8 5s.

PRICES OF HEIFERS

1797	£7 16s 6d
1804	£6
1808	£8 18s 9d and £14
1816	£3 19s
1817	£6 (each for several)
1818	£5 17s 9d (each for several)
1819	£11 18s 9d (average each of several).

PRICES OF COWS WITH CALVES

1799	£9 9s – cow and calf
1804	£12 – fat cow and calf
1808	£10 12s 6d – cow and calf
1808	£18 18s – cow and calf
1809	£14 – heifer in calf
1818	£10 6s – cow and calf
1818	£10 2s – cow and calf
1819	£12 15s – cow and calf

PRICES OF CALVES

1795	£2 6s 4d – each, for fat calves
1797	16s and 15s
1798	18s
1798	£1 1s – a Jersey, at Plymouth
1799	£1 and 16s
1799	£2 8s – a fat calf
1808	£6 3s – for two fat calves.

PRICES OF BULLOCKS, STEERS, OXEN

| 1791 | £7 1s – each for fat oxen |
| 1791 | £7 10s – each for oxen |

1795	£12 9s 4d – each for fat steers
1804	£14 14s – each for steers
1805	£12 16s 3d – each for fat bullocks
1808	£19 10s – each for steers
1816	£1 15s – each for steers
1816	£4 17s – a steer
1816	£10 3s – each for fat bullocks
1817	£12 2s 6d – a bullock
1818	£13 10s – a bullock
1816	£4 17s – a steer
1820	£13 10s – each for steers.

PRICES OF (PRESUMABLY) DRAUGHT OXEN

1804	£20 10s – pair of oxen
1804	£23 – pair of oxen
1804	£26 – for two oxen
1804	£30 – pair of oxen
1808	£21 – each, for several
1810	£22 – each, for several
1819	"Sold Leader Ox (with a garland round his neck) at Lanreath Fair" £27 10s

PRICES OF SHEEP

1789	£1 1s and 15s each for ewes
1790	October, £22 17s for 22 wether sheep
1790	August, £4 17s 6d for 8 hogg sheep
1791	£1 and £1 1s 4d each for fat sheep
1795	£1 10s each for fat ewes
1798	December, 16s 3d each for wether sheep
1799	August, £1 5s each for wether sheep
1803	April, £1 6s for a sheep
1803	November, £1 6s and £1 4s 6d each for wethers
1815	£2 13s 6d each for wethers
1806	£1 9s each for ewes
1808	£1 17s each for wether ewes
1810	£2 7s 7½d each for wethers
1815	£2 13s 6d each for wethers
1816	£1 7s for a sheep

1816	£1 10s 8d each for ewes
1818	October, £1 17s for sheep
1819	February, £2 2s for sheep
1819	£1 17s each for fat ewes.

PRICE OF RAMS

1794	£4 3s
1797	May, £2 3s 4d
1804	£4
1816	£4 10s

PRICE OF LAMBS

1791	11s each
1794	July, 9s 7½d each
1795	11s each for fat lambs
1799	January, £2 2s
1799	August, 14s to butcher
1808	16s 6d each
1810	April, £1 each

PRICES OF DONKEYS AND MULES

1799	£11 11s each for mules
1804	£5 5s for two donkeys
1808	£3 for an ass
1818	£3 3s for a jackass

I do not propose to comment upon these prices of animals – the ages and qualities of which may, of course, have accounted for much of the variation in price – or upon the prices of the following list of oddments beyond calling attention to the curiously large range in the price of bricks.

PRICES OF TIMBER, Etc.

1788	Best red deals, 10 feet by 1½ inches at 1s 10d
1788	10 feet oars at 2s each
1788	22 feet oars at 2s 6d each
1789	24 feet oars at 3s each
1789	16 feet oars at 1s 9d each

Sale of Oak trees in 1804 -

           100 for £84
            73 for £71
            80 for £30
           100 for £92
           126 for £100
            94 for £128
            69 for £85
            20 for £18
           ‾‾‾   ‾‾‾
Totals.. 662   £658

PRICES OF BRICKS

1786   5s 6d per 100 and 4s 6d
1786   £1 16s per 1,000 (2,000 bought)
1791   5s 6d per 100
1796   6s per 100
1802   £1 15s per 1,000
1803   7s 6d per 100
1804   7s 6d and 8s per 100
1804   £3 5s per 1,00 (in December)
1808   8s per 100
1819   £1 18s per 1,000
1819   7s 6d per 100

PRICES OF ODD ITEMS

1789   A scythe 4s 6d
1781   Barrel of tar, £1 8s
1820   Pitch 4s per pound
1783   Resin (in privateer's prize) £12 5s to £12
        15s per ton
1814   Hay £3 10s per ton
1781   "Cathridge" paper, 1s 3d per quire .

*   *   *   *   *

A few prices of weapons and other requisites
for privateers I reserve for a later section.
*   *   *   *   *

Lastly there are the prices of clothes and furniture etc. The clothes, unfortunately, are for the most part not comparable with those of which prices were quoted in the Records of Talland: and one can only say that shoes and mere hats – as distinct from those, perhaps beavers, of high quality – seem to have cost about the same as half a century earlier. The cotton shirt was far dearer than the Talland parish shirts: but those were, no doubt, of far commoner material.

PRICES OF CLOTHES AND MATERIALS

1782	Shoes 8s (one or two pairs?)
1786	"Shoes for Miss Trelawny" 3s
1787	Man's boots 14s 6d per pair
1789	Women's shoes 7s and 7s 6d (two pairs in each case?)
1793	Workman's shoes 5s
1783	A hat 13s 6d
1788	A hat £1 1s (for Job himself?)
1789	Two hats for young Eastcott £1 6s
1791	A hat 3s
1796	A man's hat 3s
1808	A hat £1 8s
1809	A hat for Job £1 9s
1810	A hat for Job £1 4s
1789	A great coat 9s 6d (for a boy?)
1805	A coat for workman £1 6s 8d
1796	Trousers 6s, Waistcoat 13s 6d, Cotton Shirt 5s 6d. Handkerchief 1s. Tailor's bill for a skipper.
1795	Suit of clothes for a boy (apparently a page or servant) £2 9s
1794	A riding habit £5 10s
1793	Gloves 7d per pair
1793	12 pairs of gloves – from Guernsey! – for Miss Eastcott at 2s per pair.
1807	Silk handkerchiefs 5s 3d
1794	Fine muslin from Guernsey 5s per ell

1783	Cloth 10s and 11s per yard
1802	Holland 1s 11d per yard
1804	Irish linen 4s 2d per yard
1790	A portmanteau £1 9s.

PRICES OF FURNITURE AND UTENSILS

1785	12 chairs £12 12s. Bedstead and hangings £15 4s 6d. Eight-day Clock £9 13s 6d. Card table £1 13s.
1786	Tea urn (for Trelawne) £4
1815	Tea kettle for schooner 17s less credit 2s 10d for old kettle.
1782	Six knives and forks for privateer "Swallow" 4s 6d the lot.
1791	Bought on Sir Harry's account for St. Allen's -

4 cloam basins at 10d each
4 smaller ditto at 5d each
12 plates at 2d each
2 dishes at 1s 4d each
2 dishes at 1s 2d each
2 dishes at 4d each
6 tumblers at 3½d each
2 salts at 3½d each
1 mug at 1s
2 butter boats 6d each
12 knives and forks 18s
Steel snuffers and stand 5s 8d

The crockery and glass being cheap and forks were exactly twice as expensive as those bought for the "Swallow".

* * * * *

There are two definite accounts for printing. In 1795 it cost 16s for 200 handbills advertising premises to let, and in 1804 10s for 100 handbills advertising Trelawny Barton to let.

TRAVELLING EXPENSES

There are various debits to Sir Harry Trelawny for the travelling expenses of his sons on their return to school. Thus after the summer holidays in 1797 Hamelin received £6 14s for his journey to London, and William Lewis £6 6s: whilst a year later £7 7s were given to the latter. There are other examples, two in 1796 for instance, of the £6 6s allowance: so I incline to think that this was the recognised cost, and that the £7 7s included a tip. In 1804, however, another son, Jonathan, was given £8 2s for his journey to London. Unfortunately we have no means even of guessing how much was spent on actual transport, and how much on food, and possibly beds, en route: and we are not told whether the boys travelled by coach or by post chaise. It certainly would seem reasonable to infer that these schoolboys travelled by stage coach: but other records prove that the fares by coach would have been only about two guineas each instead of six. In 1800 coach hire – clearly from London – to Plymouth for two inside passengers and one outside cost altogether £5 2s 6d: while a single fare – clearly from London – to Bristol was £1 5s, and to Portsmouth £1. The Bristol and Portsmouth fares were thus at the rate of 2½d and 2¾d per mile respectively; while the Plymouth fares averaged nearly 1¾d per mile – perhaps 2d inside and a trifle over 1½d outside. On the other hand chaise hire and driver from Lostwithiel to Falmouth – probably for two people at any rate – cost £3 in 1818, when prices were probably higher than twenty years earlier: and when Job and Mrs Braddon journeyed from Polperro to Launceston in 1812 they paid £1 6s for half of a chaise – not a post chaise I presume. It seems probable therefore that the Trelawny boys made the journey to London by post chaise, and that six guineas covered all cost of transport, turnpikes, and meals, and one night's rest at least on the way.

In 1800 it cost 5s for "a horse to ride to Torpoint" from Polperro, and presumably back – a distance of about twenty-two miles each way. For that date the charge seems very high by comparison with what could be made out as the cost of horse hire from the Records of Talland which seemed to suggest a charge of 2s 6d per horse "for a journey to any town at a distance of twelve to twenty miles" until about 1808, and twice as much very soon after 1808. Perhaps the cost varied with the quality of the steed.

I subjoin two general bills of costs for travelling and hotel expenses, the one rendered by the presumed employee of Job 's and the other that of Job's journey to Launceston with Mrs Braddon.

March 7, 1798 –		
Paid the boots	0	4
Paid Christopher Beer...	0	6
Paid for my breakfast.....	0	6
Paid for dinner............	1	0
Porter.......................	0	3
Passage.....................	0	3
Gave Jacob Beer (-?) worth to drink.....................	1	0
Paid Mr Hooper for the horses and a glass of grog	4	1
Turnpike	0	2
	8	1

The "passage" was clearly a ferry: the payment for horses cannot have been for horse-hire if the journey was to Plymouth: and Jacob

Beer was one of the smuggling fraternity. No further explanation seems needed.

The hotel bill for Job and Mrs Braddon was as follows:-

Dinner bill..................	17	6
3 teas........................	4	6
Neguss (sic!)...............	2	0
Maid and Boots............	3	0
2 beds........................	2	0
Ostler........................	1	6

It is a striking fact that the payment for service was half as much again as that for beds.

The actual travelling cost, in addition to twenty shillings for half the chaise and 1s 6d for the ostler, was 1s 9d and 4½d for turnpike tolls, and 6s for "Webb's bill for horses" – I can only suppose for stabling and feeding them: but we badly need more explanation of the expenses of this journey.

*   *   *   *   *

It is very maddening that, although Job regularly at every year-end debited each client with expenses of postage, and although he must surely have kept some postage-book or in some way have kept account of postage expenses incurred, no definite data whatever remain except the two records that in 1789 a letter to London cost 6d, and that in 1796 postage to London – for one letter, as I presumed – cost 1s. In the Records of Talland, while there were many entries of payments for postage, there were only four telling us how much a letter to a given place cost; and there was the same apparently arbitrary variation as in the two examples just quoted.

COST OF SCHOOLING.

There are records of the cost of two – if not three – very different types of schooling. In the period 1790-1793 the Eastcott girls paid Miss James £3 12s 4½d and £2 13s 6d respectively for – presumably – six months' education: and I suppose that the one took "extras" which other did not. In 1804 John Quiller's executors were debited to "school bill for your daughter at Miss Coleses, Duloe at Christmas last £3 14s." In June 1807, the bill for "schooling" was £9: in May 1808, it was £10 – and in July 1808 it was £20 for board and schooling. It is very difficult to harmonize these charges. It looks as though Miss Coles divided the year in to three terms, and charged £9 or £10 per term for education, and £10 additionally for boarders. This interpretation would fit pretty well but for the low charge in 1804: and one is left wondering whether that was for part only of a term, or whether "extras" accounted for the increase from £3 14s to £9 or £10 per term. Another possible interpretation is that Miss Coles charged by the half-year, and that the payment in May, 1808, was fore the half-year ending December 1807: and in this case the 1804 payment was probably for part only of the half year. It is noticeable that more was spent on the education of John Quiller's daughter than on that of the two Eastcott girls even taken together, although their father had been rector of Lansallos, and they probably ranked as of "the county".

When we turn to the bills paid by Job for the Trelawny boys at Westminster School we find, of course, a very different scale of charges. I will tabulate my extracts first, and then discuss their interpretation: and in the tabulation I will put together all those referring to Jonathan Trelawny, and then those referring to William Lewis.

June, 1796. £25 to Rev. – Glass "for Mr Jonathan's schooling".

December, 1796. £245 remitted to Lady Trelawny in London probably included school fees for both boys.

May, 1797. £50 to Dr Glass.

July, 1797. "To the Rev. Mr Dodd his bill for Board and Schooling for Mr Jonathan Trelawny in full £57 3s 0d.

September, 1797. "To remittance to the Rev. George Henry Glasse £78 11s 8d" (for Jonathan?).

August, 1798. £50 to Lady Trelawny "to pay Mr Jonathan's bill for schooling" and a bill for shopgoods.

September, 1796. William Lewis' schoolbills £49 5s 9d.

March, 1797. To Mrs M. Clough on account of her bill for William Lewis's board, etc, £30: and again May, 1797. £30 to her.

September, 1797. William Lewis's "Board etc, at Westminster" £62 5s.

January, 1798. £53 7s for W. L.

July, 1798. To Rev. Dodd, due to late Mrs Clough, for W. L's board and education £53 13s.

January, 1799. W. L's last bill for board and schooling £80 8s 6d.

There was also an apparently special payment in May, 1797 "to J. Goldsmith for tuition to Mr William Lewis £13 0s 0d". I infer that this was for extra coaching: but we have no indication whatever of the number of hours of coaching for which the sum of £13 was paid.

Now how are we to interpret these entries? The first question to be answered is whether the school year was divided into two halves with two payments or into three terms with three. The fact that the boys returned to school in September seemed pretty decisive against the division into half-years: the dates of payment can be harmonized with division into three terms – subject to the supposition that, though fees were normally payable in advance, they were often actually paid at the end of the term or even later: and finally, on consulting a book of reference, I gathered that the division of the year into three terms had come into vogue at public schools before the date in question. Subject to these conclusions we must infer that board and education at Westminster cost from £50 to £80 a term – apparently about £170 to £180 a year – ie. this school was fully as expensive before 1800 as the average public school in 1914. This was so astonishing discovery to me that I wrote to Westminster School enquiring whether such charges were normal at the close of the eighteenth century. In reply Mr A. H. Stenning wrote me that he knew of no records of school expenses at this period; but that the Trelawny payments "seemed very high". He kindly sent me for comparison the subjoined bill for Lord George Germain's son from 3rd June to 3rd December, 1776 – copied from the Associated Archaeological Societies' Reports and papers.

	£	s	d
Six months' board........................	12	10	0
Quarterly articles.........................	1	4	0
Extra expenses			
A bed to himself.................	2	2	0
Paid to the Abbey..............	0	1	0
Paid to the school..............	0	1	0
Sending to his apothecary......	0	2	0
Pair Buckles......................	0	0	9
Allowance money, 15 weeks			
at 6d....................	0	7	6
11 weeks at 1s..........	0	11	0

Bills paid.........................	1	10	7
Christmas fees...................	9	9	0
Mr Hume 6 months private			
Tuition...................	5	5	0

£33 3 10

It will be observed that in 1776 there were two half years, not three terms; and that the actual cost per year – if we exclude the private tuition and assume that there was no summer correlative of the Christmas fees – was only between forty and fifty pounds. The Telawny bills, therefore, remain unintelligible. Mr Stenning was unable to say at what date the change from two half-year to three terms was made. Incidentally he mentioned that Sir Harry's eldest son, John, was admitted to the school in January, 1788. John was the sailor son who has been mentioned in an earlier section.

Then only remaining item that I have noted is that in July, 1803, there was a payment of £25 to one Plummer for his expense with Jonathan Trelawny at Oxford: but the record is practically useless, as we do not know what Plummer did.

SOME LOCAL RENTS.

In an address to the Surveyors' Institution on 12th November, 1928, and in a letter to the Times early in February this year, Mr C. B. Fisher, president of the Surveyors' Institution, made a strong appeal for the preservation of documents "which would illustrate the enclosure of open fields, the growth and break-up of large estates, and fluctuations in the size of farms and rents". I have extracted from Job's books what I could find about the rents of farms: but these gleanings are pitiable compared with the harvest that might have been reaped if the rentals of the various manors possessed by Trelawny and one or two other clients of Job's had been preserved as those four of Raphiel have been. Too probably all these invaluable records perished in that bonfire – if they were not returned periodically by Job to the lords of the manors. The trouble is that normally rents were paid at the Court Leet, and Job simply credited the total to his client in his day book and ledger – all details appearing, no doubt, in the rental; so that the rent of any farm is noted separately in his daybook only when it was paid in arrear, ie. after the Court. Fortunately, however, in No. 4 we have the rents of the Eastcott properties to increase the otherwise scanty list: and these records are free from an ambiguity that has troubled me about some of the others. This trouble is that in certain cases I have felt uncertain whether the rent paid out of court was for the year or half-year or even occasionally simply a part payment on account: but in the subjoined table I have indicated any such uncertainty that I could not finally resolve. The remarks previously made – in the list of tenants – as to the dates attached apply to the following rents also.

Rents of Mrs Eastcott's properties.
Mortha. Before (?) 1777 to 1786 (and later?) £27 yearly
Mortha. 1788 to 1796 (and later?) £33 yearly.
Mortha. At least as early as 1806, £62 yearly.
Mortha. Before (?) 1815, £55 16s yearly. (in the first period £2 in all were remitted because the house was not built for two years).
Colman's (in Lansallos). Before (?) 1778 to 1782, £48 yearly.
Treweers. Before (?) 1778 to 1779, £25 yearly.
Treweers. 1780 to 1786 (and later?) £22 7s 6d yearly.

Treweers. Before 1792 to 1803 (and later?), £23 yearly.

Treweers. Before (?) 1808, £49 10s yearly.

Treweers. From 1812, £60 yearly.

(Fiddick having refused to sign the counterpart, when the lease was already made out to him at £49 10s, the farm was let to another man at £60).

Longcombe. Before (?) 1776 to November, 1785, £11 5s yearly.

Longcombe. May, 1786, to 1790 (and later?) £11 yearly.

Longcombe Mills. Before (?) 1797 to 1804 (and later?) £12 yearly.

Chestlands. Before (?) 1778 to 1780, £11 yearly7.

Chestlands. 1780 to 1784 (and later?) £5 10s yearly.

"The Warren, etc." Before (?) 1778 to March 1783, £11 1s yearly.

"The Warren, etc." March 1783 to 1797 (and later?) £6 yearly.

High Park. Before (?) 1779 to ---? £3 1s yearly

High Park. Before 1797, £3 19s yearly.

"The Island at Looe" alias "The Island House at East Looe" 1778, £8 8s yearly. 1798, £8 yearly.

Lime Kilns at Polperro. From ---? To March 1780, £12 yearly.

Lime Kilns at Polperro. March, 1780, to 1786 (and later?) £8 yearly.

The New Inn. 1780 to 1783, £11 5s yearly.

The New Inn. 1784 to end 1786, £11 yearly.

The New Inn. 1788 to 1790 (and later?) £10 yearly.

The New Inn. 1794 to end 1796, £9 yearly.

The New Inn. 1797, £13 10s for year (?).

The New Inn. 1797, £20 yearly.

(The expenses of re-letting the Inn at the end of 1796 were £2 5s 10d).

Many, at any rate, of the following were Trelawny property.

Little Larnack. 1802, £60 yearly.

Catherine (?) Park (?) let with preceding (?) 1802, £15 yearly.

Moiety of Little Tratford. 1803, £15 yearly.

Trelaske and Wayland. 1803, £15 yearly

Trelaske. 1816, £40 yearly.

Hendersick. 1803, £126 yearly.

Hendersick. 1819, £210 yearly.

Killiow. Before (?) 1781-1783, £19 yearly, for half of it.

Killiow. 1784, Possibly for the whole farm, £35 yearly.

Tregarrick. 1803, £100 yearly.

Trendaway. 1803, £70 yearly.

Perglaze. Before (?) 1807 to 1812 at least, £35, yearly I suppose.

Polpever. 1804, £39, yearly I suppose.

Polpever. 1807, £25 8s yearly??

Polmartin. 1804, £60 yearly.

Portallow. Before (?) 1806 to 1812 (and later?), £45 yearly.

Portallow. 1817 apparently, £46 10s yearly, with poor's rates allowed off.

Portallow. 1819, £46 10s yearly.

Portallow. 1820, £42 yearly. Perhaps nett after deducting rates.

Looe Island. 1799, £8 yearly.

Looe Island. 1814, £15, yearly I suppose.

Merrifield. 1818, £35 yearly ? or half-yearly?

Port Looe. 1812, £100 yearly.

* * * * *

On sundry of the foregoing properties Conventionary or Chief (ie. ground) Rents were paid to the actual freeholders. Thus there was a Conventionary Rent of £1 5s 4d on Portallow, and a Chief Rent of one penny on Pelean – which latter, however, does not appear above. Eastcott paid a Chief Rent of tenpence on "the island in East Looe" to the Mayor: and his sisters paid a Conventionary Rent of 6s 8d to the Buller family on the New Inn.

We have also the rents of a few cottages, only one or two of which, however, are identifiable. In the 1778 to 1786 period the Eastcotts let a "dwelling house" to William George at £1 10s yearly, another to Joseph Kendall at £2 2s, a third to Joseph Pearce at £2 12s 6d, two others also at £2 12s 6d each, and Trelawne Cross House at £1 3s. As already noted, Colman's House was let to Lansallos Parish for many years at £3 3s. We know in addition that in 1797 John Libby was renting a house at Crumplehorn for £1 11s 6d yearly; and that in 1790 Robert Soady was paying Job either the same rent or £1 10s for his dwelling house. Mrs Eastcott also received a rent of apparently £2 2s yearly for Gresson Pool House, which I take to be the cottage(s) in Pelynt parish between Blue Gate and Ashen Cross. The entry from which I calculate the rent at £2 2s is as follows, under the date April, 1782. "Cash recd. of Mr John Sargent for ¼ (ie. 3 months?) Rent of Gresson Pool House viz the Parishioners' ½ of do. Sir Harry Trelawny agreeing to pay the other ½ for Notwell – 5/3." No doubt this entry was perfectly intelligible to all those concerned; but I had to consider carefully what it meant as datum for the yearly rent.

Finally from September, 1787 to 1790 anyhow "the field at Crumplehorn" was let at £6 per year – the tithe thereon being 15s, 15s and 16s 6d respectively in these three years.

* * * * *

In addition to the foregoing data there are those

already given in the Rentals of Landaviddy for a large number of cottages, etc, and several farms.

TAXES AND RATES.

This section will not be lengthy: but it seemed worth while to extract and tabulate some data on local taxes and rates. In October 1787 the assessed taxes on Trelawne for the half year were:

> On 68 windows, £7 9s 6d
> On 2 men servants, £1 5s
> On 3 women servants, 15s
> On a four-wheeled carriage, £3 10s
> On 4 horses, £1.

making a total of £13 19s 6d, ie. £27 19s for the year. Unfortunately I seem to have no note of the land tax on Trelawne at this date: but in October, 1797, the half-year's taxes on land, house, windows, servants, horses and dogs were £20 11s 2d – equivalent to £41 2s 4d yearly – and in April, 1798, the half-year's "assessed" taxes were £26 10s 7d or at a rate of £53 0s 6d yearly. In 1803 the year's taxes on windows and servants and horses amounted to £57 5s 3d; and in 1804 the land tax alone was £21 12s. If there had been no change from 1803 to 1804, the inference seems to be that the total taxation had risen from £41 in 1797 to nearly £79 in 1803. Next we have data of the "assessed" taxes for a series of years: and it seems pretty clear that these did not include land tax, and that the figures therefore must be compared with the earlier £27 19s of 1787 and the £53 0s 6d of 1798. These assessed taxes were

> In 1805 £65 1s apparently.
> In 1806 £49 7s.
> In 1807 £57 2s 5d.
> In 1808 £55 7s.
> In 1809 £60
> In 1815 £63 0s 6d apparently.

In 1818 £63 (about)
In 1819 £61 13s (about)
In 1820 £62 11s (if no change in the second half year).

It looks rather as if Sir Harry reduced his taxes in 1806 by building up some windows or decreasing the number of his horses or servants, unless "assessed" taxes were slightly lowered for a time in view of new taxes being imposed. As early as 1803 or 1804 a property tax of 1s in the pound was levied on incomes: and in 1806 this was increased to 2s.

The land-tax on Lansallos Rectory was £16 10s yearly between 1780 and 1790, but £17 5s 8d from 1806 onwards to 1814 – and presumably later. The tax for 1805 was either £16 4s 4d or £17 8s 4d.

I was much amused at finding that one of the taxes imposed during the earlier war with France was a tax on hairpowder at a guinea per head. Here are several examples from Job's account with Sir Harry.

April, 1797. Four hairpowder licences, £4 4s.
April, 1798. "To Hairpowder Licences for My Lady, Sir Harry, Miss Trelawny and James Rendle, £4 4s."
July, 1800. Sir Harry's and "James's" licences, £1 1s each.
James Rendle was obviously either coachman or footman.

It seems to me that a modern Chancellor of the Exchequer might well take a hint from this precedent: for, if he would impose an ad valorem stamp tax of 100 per cent on powders and paints for the face, he would undoubtedly collect some millions from this source and be enabled to lower some other and far more oppressive tax.

The licence to use armorial bearings cost two guineas in 1800 e.g: and in February 1790 Sir Harry was debited "To Passport from the Secretary of State to travel through France £2 13s 6d". A passport now costs 7s 6d; and before the war only 2s 6d.

* * * * *

There are a few records of local rates in my notes. In June, 1796, the Highway Rate on Port Looe came to ten shillings: and in 1812 this rate was sevenpence in the pound. In 1786 the Poor Rate on "the Island in Looe" – ie. presumably the Island House – for two years was only 16s 6d: in 1798 the half-year's rate on Port Looe was only £1 6s 8d; and in April, 1797, the half-year's rate even on Trelawne was £7 13s 4d. In the course of twenty years the Poor's Rate on Lansallos Rectory was trebled: but it must be remembered that this rate was levied on tithes, and that these tithes increased nearly twofold during the period in question: but the general increase in the cost of relieving the poor may well have been over fifty per cent. These rates on Lansallos Rectory are tabulated below.

1799	£28 yearly.
1805	£35 yearly.
1806	£45 yearly.
1807	£18 for second half-year.
1808	£24 for second half-year.
1809	£46 10s for whole year.
1810	£49 for whole year.
1811	£50 for whole year.
1812	£24 for first half-year.
1813	£61 10s for whole year.

1814	£57 for whole year.
1815	£49 10s for whole year.
1816	£54 for whole year.
1818	£36 for half-year.
1819	£78 for whole year.
1820	£42 for half-year.

WAGES OF FARM WORKERS.

In my attempt to trace the history of wages in this part of Cornwall from the Talland Records I had to lament the almost complete lack of any data covering agricultural workers and unskilled labourers between 1778, when they still got 1s per day, and 1829, when they were getting 1s 6d. There was just one record of a man getting 1s 2d in 1792 for work with a mason; and there was the possibility that the Sexton got 1s 1d or 1s 2d per day in 1795 and 1796 for extra and unskilled work.

From these meagre data I provisionally and rather doubtfully inferred that between 1778 and 1792 the day's wage had gone up from 1s to 1s 2d; but I could feel no certainty about this inference and there was no indication whatever of the date at which the pay had gone up to 1s 6d. Job's books afford us a wealth of data for filling up the gaps in the story and tracing chronologically the rise in wages.

In 1783 Joseph Kendall got 1s per day as agricultural labourer; and William Bunt got the same for "work" and the same for carrying dung; but Thomas Wise got 17s 6d for fifteen days' work, ie. 1s 2d per day; and in 1784 our old acquaintance – of the Talland Records – Cornelius Teague, also got 2s 4d for two days work. Thus we have the certain fact that at least as early as August, 1783, the wage had gone up to 1s 2d for some men. It was till, however, by no means the fixed daily pay of every farm worker and unskilled labourer, or even of any given same man under all conditions: for in 1786 Kendall got 1s per day for four days at Mortha, but 1s 2d per day for eighteen at Longcombe. So, too, in 1787 a man got 1s per day for three days' hedging; and in 1789 a man was paid 1s per day for his work: whereas, also in 1789, John Jago got 1s 2d; and another, who got 1s 2d, "finding himself in syder", was paid 1s 6d for harvesting.

In 1791 Robert Soady got 12s for ten days' tillage and harvesting, or an average of 1s 2½d per day: but we do not know whether he was paid at 1s 6d for four days' harvesting, and at 1s for six days' tillage, or how the total was made up. He or another was paid at 1s for quenching lime, and at 1s for fetching lime; and a man paid by the year got 1s per day. In 1792 a lime-worker of some sort got 15s 6d for fourteen days' work, or about 1s 1½d per day, and on another occasion 1s 2d. In 1793 one man got 1s per day for work not specified; "a man in garden" 1s 2d, and an agriculturalist 1s 2d; but one man got 1s 6d per day for some sort of work.

Now, the payment of 1s 6d in 1789 for harvesting is neither puzzling nor perhaps significant, since notoriously men often work considerably over-time at harvesting and get special pay. But this payment at 1s 6d in 1793 is a puzzle unless it be significant as the first indication of the second and greater increase that was so soon to follow the rise from 1s to 1s 2d, though even this was not yet stabilised. In 1794 a man "at wood" got 1s 1d; perhaps the same man at other work 1s; but another man 1s 2d.

On the basis of these data, extending over twelve years, we can safely conclude that the day's wage had risen from 1s to 1s 2d for those who could get it, and that the Talland record of 1792 was correctly interpreted. The Talland entries had indicated that wages were in a very fluid condition during the last decade of the seventeenth century, had remained so up to 1720, and were still variable up to 1745: and I could not feel certain whether the variations about 1693 indicated rising or falling wages. Here, a hundred years later, we find similar variation, but in this case there is certainty that the variation was due to a rise. Moreover, the period of fluctuation was of far shorter duration; and about or actually before the day's wage had been really stabilized at 1s 2d, another rise began – conditioned, no doubt, by the increased cost of living and especially of bread, the price of which in 1795 was twice as much as in 1785; whilst in 1800 and in several later years it was far higher still.

Now, in 1795 one man got 1s 2d per day; another got 1s 3d for cutting up woods, but 1s 4d for fencing as also for cutting coppice: whereas a third got 1s 4d for repairing the road, but 1s 2d for other work. In 1796 a man got 1s 2d as lime-burner's assistant apparently; and another 1s 2d for other work, whilst on the same day a third got 1s 4d for cutting wood apparently; and many others also got 1s 4d. Among these last was Joseph Kendall, whose job was that of fencing woods and removing an old gateway: but on another occasion in the same year he received 1s 7d. Conceivably, for this abnormal pay, he may have worked a little overtime. In this same year, too, I find 1s 6d per day for sowing, and the same for loading a vessel: but in December, 1797, Job paid John Libby only at 1s 4d for 2½ days' work.

In this same year too, I find payment of 1s 6d per day for hedging: and from 1802 to 1820 there are sheaves of examples of this payment to farm labourers; and the wage was now so definitely stabilized that it would be absurdly superfluous to quote examples.

Thus we may sum up by saying that not later than in 1783 the day wage of farm workers and unskilled labourers went up from 1s to 1s 2d for some men or for some of their work; that in 1795 and 1796 it varied from 1s 2d to 1s 3d or 1s 4d or even 1s 6d; and that in 1802 it was already stabilized at 1s 6d, and probably had been so in 1800 or between 1796 and 1800. The fact that in 1794-5 Eastcott paid John Burn only 21s a month cannot be set against this conclusion, for we do not know what work Burn really did, or whether he was an old man, or whether he received additionally any food or other payment in kind. When we find, however, that in 1800 Sir Harry Trelawny paid William Langmead only £21 yearly, ie. 1s 4d per day plus 4s yearly we must admit that the wage of this regular labourer lagged behind the new standard – unless he got perquisites in addition. I may add that in 1803 a man was paid 2s an acre for mowing barley and oats, but 2s 6d an acre for cutting hay.

A record of 1807 rather puzzled me: for Charles Edwards – evidently someone in agriculture - got 10s per week, ie. 1s 8d per day. Possibly he was a bailiff or foreman at Killiow.

There are records of boys' wages which are of very little value, because a boy may have been of any age from ten to sixteen or more; but for what they may be worth, here they are: - In 1796 a boy got 3d per day; in 1803 and 1804 a boy got 6d per day, no doubt for farm work; in 1807 there are payments of 6d to one boy, and at 3½d to another, who was paid quarterly; in 1808 of 8d to one and 4d to another; and in 1810 of 9d; while in 1816 we find a boy at 6d per day. We must infer that these boys were of very varying ages. In 1812 Job gave Harry Tregair, junior, 21s "on his going off from Killiowe Farm". Harry's father was one of Job's permanent workers on the farm: and we know from the 1808 Rental of Raphiel that Harry would be 17 years old in 1812. The record seems to me rather noteworthy.

It will be convenient to clear off a few odd payments connected with agriculture before passing to the wages of artisans. In 1798 mole-catchers were paid 2d per mole, but only 1½d at Port Looe. In 1799 five moles caught "in the garden" brought in 3d each; but in 1800 there is a payment at 2d.

* * * * *

I have also a record that in 1795 Job "paid Mark Rowe 4 days carrying rubbish 9/6", and three weeks later "paid Mark Rowe 5 Days work 12/6". Now, on the face of it, this is all hopeless nonsense: for, at a date when the labourer's wage was 1s or 1s 2d per day, Mark Rowe certainly did not get 2s 6d. The obvious explanation is that Mark was paid for the use of a horse or horses also. Accordingly, as he got 1s or 1s 2d for himself, there would have been 1s 4½d or 1s 2½d per day for horse-hire on the four days' job, and 1s 6d or 1s 4d on the other. The Talland Records indicated probably 9d per day for horse-hire in 1779: so Mark probably used two horses at nearly or about 9d each.

ARTISANS' WAGES

Now let us consider the wages of artisans, and, firstly, of carpenters. In 1786 there is the entry: "Paid Mrs Parne 6 days her husband 9s". The context suggests that the payment may well have been for carpenter's work; and I am fairly sure that "Parne" was simply an alias for carpenter Pearn – probably an ancestor of the present carpenter of that name. This gives a wage of 1s 6d per day to a carpenter at a date when some farm workers had secured 1s 2d; and thus there was the same difference – though not the same proportion – between the rates of pay as in 1742, when the labourer got 1s and the carpenter 1s 4d, as shown on the Talland Records.

On the other hand, there is the definite statement that in 1794 "a carpenter" was paid at 1s 2d per day; but this seems unintelligible unless the "carpenter" in question was really, not a duly-trained man who had served his apprenticeship, but simply a handy man, ranking for pay as an unskilled labourer, but clever at rough carpentry. If this be the explanation, that "carpenter" has had successors up to this day in Polperro! In 1804 a man was paid 2s per day for work at a barge. If he was a carpenter, the pay was exactly in the old proportion now that the labourer was getting 1s 6d. It is most disappointing that so very little precise information can be found about the pay of carpenters, although these workers were so very much in evidence in Job's books.

I have not taken in order of dates the record of 1782 that eight men got 2s 7½d per day each, four others 2s 6d, and three boys 1s 3d, for work on the "Swallow" privateer: for I think that they must have been specialised workmen, not carpenters, or else that there was feverish haste to fit out the vessel, and that abnormal wages were paid, possibly included expenses of lodging for strangers temporarily imported.

THE PAY OF MASONS.

The information about masons' pay is also very unsatisfactory. On a loose receipted bill of 1810 a mason's wage is given positively at 1s 3d per day, but this is obvious nonsense. Whatever be the explanation, and whatever blunder may have been made, a mason undoubtedly was not paid 3d per day less than a labourer. In this same year some man got 2s per day for "hedging", and one must infer that this "hedging" was masonic and not agricultural. In 1810, too, Hodge was paid 2s per day for two days "in the garden", and for five days "making the road, etc.", and again for four days "in the garden and six about the quays", and later in the year he was employed for four weeks at the same rate, whilst another man got also 2s per day for work in the garden and about the kiln. I infer that both men were masons and that the work "in the garden" was not horticultural but masonic. In this case the pay at 2s per day agrees with that of carpenters.

I had previously interpreted an entry in the Talland Records as indicating that the mason Soady got at least 2s per day in 1792; and in that case it would seem that the masons had secured their 50 per cent increase on their wages of the second and third quarters of the eighteenth century, some years earlier than the labourers achieved the same proportionate increase. If carpenters and masons were always paid the same, the latter also must apparently have passed through the stage of 1s 6d per day between 1780 and 1792, but unhappily we have no records of this.

The masons must have gained another increase within the second decade of the nineteenth century: for in 1818 Job entered 2s 6d per day to "William Hill, mason"; and this entry enables us to understand an account of 1817 which pretty certainly concerns the rebuilding of the quay – and, likely enough, repairs to the limekilns – after the terrible storm in January of that year. Various men working on this job got 2s 6d per day and others 1s 6d – the former evidently masons I think, and the latter their labourers. It seems a reasonable inference that carpenters' pay at this date had also been increased to 2s 6d, but I have no definite proof of this.

* * * * *

Two entries of 1785 may here be quoted, with the candid confession that I cannot understand the rate of pay. They are: - "To John Couch 4 days taking up and planting appletrees at Mortha 8/-" ; and "Paid Mrs (?) Couch one day myself 1/6". Why Couch should have been paid 2s when the farm labourer with luck could just get 1s 2d; and why Job paid only 1s 6d himself to – as one supposes – the same man, I cannot in the least understand. It is very curious that in the Talland Records we found abnormally high pay given to a John Couch in 1767. Was this the same man: and was he so uncommonly clever at some jobs as to secure special payment, or some local favourite who was exceptionally treated?

* * * * *

Although, as has already been shown, only the labourers' pay of 1s to 1s 2d was given to several men for jobs connected with lime, yet the actual staff at the limekilns, and also the bargees, seem to have been paid at least as highly as carpenters and masons; and it is so difficult to determine whether some of the men paid for loading and unloading barges at the kilns were the kiln men or the bargees that I propose to take the two classes together. It is, perhaps, intelligible that the bargees, qua navigators, and the kiln men qua limeburners, should have received the pay of skilled workers; but it is notable that they got the same pay even when doing the mere labourers' work of loading and unloading barges. Is there some little bit of social or economic history in the background? However that be, here are the facts as to wages per day:-

1792	To George Teague, limeburner, for "discharging culm", 2s.
1804	To a bargee 2s.
1806	To Blatchford 2s 6d (What and who was he?)
1806	To a bargee 2s 6d.
1808	To Bunt, apparently for digging clay 2s 6d.
1808	To several "about oats" 2s.
1808	To several "about culm" 2s 6d. (Clearly loading or unloading)
1808	To work about culm 2s 6d.
1808	To Rabby, work on kiln, 2s.
1808	Cutting a rock 2s. (I inferred that Rabby was a bargee and the men of the three preceding entries perhaps bargees also)
1809	For carrying lime and clearing rubbish 2s.
1809	"At the kiln" 2s.
1810	For carrying (?) culm 2s 6d.
1810	For loading and unloading culm 2s 6d.
1810	For improving the road 2s 6d.

I incline to infer, when extracting these records, that men, who usually got 2s per day, were paid

2s 6d for loading culm; but why did clay-digging and road improving earn this higher pay too?

Another entry of 1810 seems to imply that a man got 3s 6d per day for fifteen days at lime-burning. This, I suppose, was special and only occasional or intermittent work; but the pay seems relatively very high.

The quay records of 1817 include 2s per day to men "carrying culm"; and when extracting these accounts I thought – whether correctly or erroneously – that some of those at 2s 6d were kiln men.

*   *   *   *   *

In 1793 a charge for sweeping six chimneys was 5s 6d. How were they swept? An Act to regulate chimney-sweeping had been passed in 1789.

THE WAGES OF WOMEN.

Now let us consider the wages of women. It really helps us not at all to learn that in 1794 Job paid 19s 6d, and again £2 2s 4d to women for loading oats on a vessel; and 4s in 1796 for carrying a bargeload(!) of culm to Looe Quay; because in not one of these three cases are we told how many women were employed; but the third entry suggests that the pay was shockingly low for very heavy work. As regards work indoors, it seems that in 1788 and 1794 the pay was 6d per day for washing, in 1783 for work "in house" 4d – but no doubt with food also – and 6d in 1794 "in house". These were payments at Trelawne.

For fieldwork we have abundant records over a series of years from 1803 to 1817, besides several earlier isolated entries, which conclusively prove that there were graded and fixed rates of pay. For weeding, picking stones, digging potatoes, and work at the hay, the pay was 6d per day; and there was the same pay in 1797 for haymaking, and in 1796 for picking apples. For hoeing turnips the pay was 8d, and for reaping 1s – with a solitary entry of 6d in 1808 for harvesting. It is a pathetic record.

As for girls, I find one paid 4d per day in 1794: whilst a "little maid" got the same in 1816 and 1817 for field work.

DOMESTIC SERVANTS.

I have left to the last the wages of domestic servants, whether men or women.

In 1787 Samuel Vague was getting £7 10s per year from Sir Harry Trelawny, and in 1797 William Rendle £6 6s from Eastcott. Possibly both Vague and Rendle were coachmen. In 1798 Job debited Sir Harry with £10 18s for one year's wages, boots and hat for a manservant, probably a coachman.

There are naturally more data concerning maidservants. About 1798 Job himself was apparently employing Catherine Courtice at £3 per year, with an increase to £3 10s in the second year; and even Sir Harry paid only £3 to Jane Dyer in 1793, and £3 3s to a maid in 1795. In 1796 Eastcott was paying Elizabeth Hill only £4 4s, and Mary Medland the same in 1797 and 1798 and 1799; but he was giving £6 6s to Mary Lean in 1797 and 1798, and £6 6s to Elizabeth Grigg also in 1797, and £5 to "Phoeby" Richards in 1799. Sir Harry was paying £4 4s to Rebecca Wareham, and £6 6s to Johanna

Williams in 1797, but £5 5s to "Mary" and £6 6s to Jane Bunt in 1799. In 1800 Martha Sleeman was paid £16 16s for three years' wages at Trelawne – ie. probably £5 5s each for two years and £6 6s for the third – while Mary Maynard got £7 7s for one year. Other Trelawne wages were £6 6s to Mary Lean in 1802 but only £5 5s to "Mary Ann" in 1803, and the same to Rachel Jago in 1808.

I noticed that domestic servants seem to have been paid once a year, or exceptionally after two or three years, as in the case of Martha Sleeman; but sometimes they received part of their wages earlier on account, and the balance later.

MEN'S WAGES TABULATED.

It will, perhaps, be worth while to tabulate the joint results of the Talland Records and Job's books as to the wages of labourers and artisans, subject to the various qualifications and conditions that I have noted, and to the assumptions (a) that any determination of a carpenter's wage is valid for that of a mason at the same date, and vice-versa; (b) that the men on the roads at 1s 2d in 1693 were masons – as suggested in the Addenda to the Talland Records; (c) that Parne in 1786 was a carpenter.

LABOURERS.

1690 to 1740	10d to 1s
1740 to 1783	1s
1783 to 1794	1s to 1s 2d
1795 and 1796	1s 2d to 1s 4d or 1s 6d
Probably before 1800	1s 6d
By 1854	2s

MASONS AND CARPENTERS.

1690	1s 2d
1728 to 1783	1s 4d usually
1742 onwards	1s 4d
1786	1s 6d
1792	2s
1817	2s 6d

At a later stage of my work I found among other loose papers – to be described hereafter – various receipted bills for labour on W.L.S.T.'s Flintshire property in 1802 and 1803. From these it appears that a mason's work was paid at 2s per day, plastering and colouring and repairing slates at 2s 6d, and carpenter's work at 2s 6d. Another worker, unspecified, got also 2s 6d, and a "labourer" 2s; but this latter must obviously have been a skilled craftsman of some kind and not an unskilled labourer. Another labourer, perhaps, working under a plasterer, got only 1s 2d per day: but possibly he was a youth and not entitled to adult pay.

It is interesting to compare these Flintshire wages with those paid in Cornwall. I do not at all understand why the mason received less than the carpenter and plasterer; and I should greatly like to know whether the unspecified workman at 2s 6d was another mason.

MARINE INSURANCE.

There are a few records of the cost of insuring vessels and their cargo at a period when depredations by enemy craft were, of course, always to be feared. In 1796 the charge was two guineas per cent on the "Richard and Mary" sailing from London to Falmouth and insured for

£800; and the same premium per cent was paid on a cargo of oil sent from Plymouth to London and incurred for £450. In 1803 and again in 1804 the insurance of the brig "Richard and Mary" for a voyage from Looe to Wales and back cost £16 10s. The rate was ten or eleven times as high for voyages to Italy – and very naturally, as vessels had to run the gauntlet along both seaboards of France.

On pilchards sent in 1796 from Fowey to Venice, and insured for £800, a premium of £169, ie. at 21 per cent, was charged; while pilchards from Fowey to Naples, insured for £700, cost £169 15s – the rate in this case being at £23 12s 6d per cent. At the end of 1794 Messrs John Owen Parr, clearly insurance people, were debited £1,658 "to Total loss of the 'Three Brothers' and her cargo – Hercules Jenkins, master". As just under £270 premium had been paid, the rate was nearly 17 per cent. Incidentally, another "Three Brothers" was built or bought next year by John Quiller, father of Richard, William and John.

It is a significant fact that there are several examples in 1796 of a return of part of the premium when the vessel insured fell in with a convoy. Thus the "Richard and Mary", insured for £1,500 on the vessel and part of the cargo, fell in with a convoy near Gibraltar, and consequently a repayment of £46 16s of the premium was made, ie., the rate was reduced by over 3 per cent as on the whole voyage, whereas the reduction on the convoyed part thereof was obviously greater. One remembers that in the Great War the convoy system was at last introduced, and with success.

THE POLPERRO SMUGGLERS

Since Job is remembered chiefly as the Smugglers' Banker, it need hardly be said that his books are largely occupied during many years by entries relevant to this unlawful but once thriving industry: and from the mere accounts – ie., without any search through his correspondence for information – one can learn pretty clearly how the trade was carried on. The Polperro smugglers habitually got their supplies from Guernsey, but seem never to have traded with Jersey: and I have found only one trifling account with an Alderney firm. It is evident that the Guernsey firms gave them several months' credit: and one of course assumes that during the interval between shipping a cargo and paying for it they had to sell their goods. Except as regards odd casks of brandy, etc, etc, sold to neighbouring individuals, one can learn nothing whatever from Job's books about the disposal hereabouts of the smuggled goods: and I cannot offer even a guess about the identity and provenance of the purchasers. When, however the smugglers had sold their goods, and the time had come for paying those who had supplied them, then it was that Job functioned as the smugglers' banker. This title carries the obvious implication that the Polperro smugglers banked with him: but, with a few exceptions, they did not. His role was to receive their payments on account of the Guernsey dealers, and to remit to these: so that he was actually the Guernsey traders' banker rather than the smugglers' banker. The sums thus collected by him from the smugglers on the Guernsey accounts constitute a measure of the trade unlawfully carried on by one small fishing village: and the following figures speak for themselves:

Credited to Jersey and de Lisle –

From March 1778, to April, 1779	£1,438
From April 1779, to April, 1781	£3,192
From April 1781, to July 1782	£851
From July 1782, to end of 1783	£1,657
From July 1784, to July 1787	£1,887
From August 1787, to May 1789	£1,200

Credited to Peter de Isle –

From October 1788, to June 1791	£6,014
From July 1791, to October 1792	£5,681
From November 1792, 2nd July 1794	£6,375
From July 1794, to late August 1795	nearly £2,200

In 1796, 1797, 1798, 1799, the amounts were quite small. (It looks very much as if Peter de Lisle were the successor to Jersey and de Lisle, or as though the firm changed its or their name.)

Credited to de Jersey and Corbin –

From May 1783, to April 1788	£3,624

Credited to John Guille & Co. –

From March 1778, to July 1779	£1,991

and to de Jersey Guille and Co. (the same firm?)

from September 1779, to July 1781	£3,066

Credited to Henry Brock –

From July 1779, to May 1780	£785
From August 1780, to May 1781	£584
From August 1781, to August 1782	£324
From August 1783, to February 1786	£1,119

(The account ends unbalanced, with nearly a whole double page blank: and on this last page is "Henry Brock, Esq.," instead of "Mr Henry Brock" as before.)

Credited to (1) Peter Mourant –

From 22nd March 1778, to end of July 1779	£358

(2) Mourant and Chepwell -

From 22nd March 1778, to July 1779	£1,024
From November 1779, to July 1781	£903
From July 1782, to November 1783	£140

(3) Mourant and Combes –

From May 1782, to March 1783   £1,222

(4) Peter Mourant and Co. –

From May 1783, to the end of March 1784 £674

(William Combes was either agent for or partner in (1) and (2); for he signed a receipt for payment to (1) jointly with Peter Mourant, and signed a receipt for the payment to (2) up to July 1779, alone per procuration.)

Credited to (1) Thomas Priaulx –

From August 1778 to August 1782 –   £960

(2) de Carteret and Co., who in 1787 became de Carteret and Co.

From June 1783, to March 1784	£894
From March 1785, to March 1787	£2,927
From April 1787, to August 1787	£228
From December 1787, to July 1792	£594

(1790 and 1791 were blank years: and the account for the second half of 1792 was only £12 10s.)

From July 1793, to April 1795	£10,755
From end of April 1795 to November 1795	
	£5,500
In 1796, 1797, 1798 –	nothing
In 1799	over £1,100

Credited to Nicholas Maingy and Brothers –

From October 1778, to July 1782	£3,886
From August 1782, to June 1785	£5,022
From July 1785, to February 1792	£5,385
From March 1782, to November 1792	£1,255

(but privateering accounts were included in this account of 1792.)

From late November 1793 to 1st October 1794	
	£543
In 1795	nothing
In 1796	£200
From January 1797, to January 1799	£12,710
From January 1799, to January 1800	£13,735
From early (?) 1800 to May 1804	£13,754

From May 1804, to May 1806   only £224

In 1808, for an account of 1804   15!

    Credited to Brock Laseere Maingy & Co (in which firm Peter Maingy was included)

From November 1806, to July 1807   £753

Credited to John Lukis –

In 1790   £96

From May 1791, to December 1792   £860

From January 1793, to June 1793   £2,815

From July 1793, to end of August 1793   £422

From October 1793, to August 1794   £132

From September 1794, to end of June 1795

                                  £4,676

In remainder of 1795   nearly £1,450

In 1796   £6,199

In 1798   £2,027

In 1799   £1,706

From January 1800, to 27th November 1800

                                  £2,394

    (this sum of £2,394 was carried forward to ledger No. 36; but, as the relevant pages of this ledger are missing, we have no data for this account for several years).

From October 1804, to July 1807   Only £537

In 1808   - only £40 7s for a pipe of port wine "sent me".

    Credited to Hillary Boucault and Co. –

From January 1800, to 29th January 1802   £2,819

    (this sum was carried forward to missing pages of No. 36; and it may have been increased considerably during early 1802).

From some date in 1802 (the early part of this account being also missing), to end of March 1803   £1,952

From May 1803, to May 1805   £1,314

From June 1805, to March 1806   £455

    Credited to Thomine Moullin and Co. –

In two months of 1804   £521

From August 1805, to July 1806   £414

John Robilliard of Alderney was, no doubt, in the same way of business: but there was only a small account with him. With this solitary exception all the firms engaged in supplying the smugglers were in Guernsey – which, of course, is very appreciably nearer than Jersey. Since we must infer that Guernsey similarly supplied the smugglers of all the coastline from perhaps the Lizard to Sussex, the total entrepot trade of that small island must have been enormous.

If the foregoing figures be added, it will be found that during the twenty-two years 1778-1799 the Polperro smugglers paid these various Guernsey firms through Job, £131, 363, or an annual average of £5,971; and that during the eight years 1800-1807 they paid £25,137, or an annual average of £3,142. It is true that in the twenty-two years' total is included whatever proportion of Maingy's £1,255 in 1795 was on privateering account: but the omission of even the entire sum of £1,255 would leave the annual average above £5,900. On the other hand the total and average for the eight years 1800-1807 are definitely too low – quite likely very considerably too low – owing to the loss of pages in No. 36 with the accounts of Lukis and Hillary Boucault. In view of what has been said later I draw attention to the significant fact that the figures for 1807 are so low that, if we omit this year, the average during the seven years 1800-1806 exceeded £3,400 plus the missing accounts.

Now be it noted that all the figures aforesaid represent only the wholesale cost to the smugglers of their goods: but we do not in the least know at what price they sold them in order to cover, in addition to the prime cost, (1) the expense of their vessels, including virtual insurance against not only ordinary dangers of the sea but also the risks of capture; (2) similar virtual insurance of cargo; (3) their own profits, ie., their income from their work; and possibly (4) the risk of their own necks – since smuggling was a capital offence. If under these circumstances they sold at twice the price which they had paid, then in the twenty-two years they received over a quarter of a million sterling for smuggled goods, and in the later eight years over £50,000: but of course we do not know whether they sold at twice the cost price or at more or less. It is wonderful that during thirty years – and for how long previously? – such a volume of contraband was steadily poured into a small fishing village from a depot separated by a hundred miles of – frequently very stormy – sea.

There are various questions about these Guernsey firms which we can ask, but for answering which there are no data – unless the answers be buried somewhere in the twenty-five pounds' weight of Job's correspondence. Why do we hear nothing about the de Lisle firms and the de Carteret Priaulx after 1799; while the accounts with Maingy run through 30 years? Why did not Lukis appear sooner: why did Hillary Boucault come in so late: and why was there so little trade with the Mourant group? Did the smugglers fall out, after a time, with one firm and then another, and take their custom to some rival firm; and for any such quarrel what were the grounds: or did one Guernsey firm after another come to grief? Did each of these firms stock every kind of contraband; or did each specialize? Again, were these definite firms or legal partners; or were they only temporary associations of two or more men? Why did the personnel, or at any rate the designation, of various firms – if they were really firms – shift so much, and especially in the de Lisle, de Jersey and the Mourant groups? What happened to Henry Brock in 1786: and was he the Brock whom we find with Maingy in 1806? All such questions can be asked: but they cannot be answered from Job's daybooks and ledgers.

Next let us note some of the individual payments by Polperro smugglers. I have merely taken some examples of the large payments in order to indicate on how very large scale some of these smugglers worked. It must be distinctly understood that smaller payments were far more numerous, and that the business was not confined to a few men working on this large scale. Here then are some examples.

In 1778 and the three following years there were very heavy payments by John Baker and Co., of which I will quote only:

£344 in August, 1780, to John Guille. £162 in October, 1780 and £406 in December, 1780 to Jersey de Guille and Co.

In December, 1778, William Johns paid to Jersey and de Lisle £179: and John Quiller's payments to the same firm were:

£179 in December, 1778. £230 in February, 1779. £180 in March, 1779. £400 in May, 1779. £158 in August, 1779. £120 in September, 1779. £189 in November. ie., £1,456 in exactly twelve months.

In 1780 he paid to the account of the same firm £99 16s in January. £241 in April. £156 in July. £135 in August. £212 in September. ie., £853 in nine months.

Richard Rowett & Co. paid to Jersey de Lisle £165 12s in February, 1781. £216 in March, 1781.

John Quiller paid to Maingy £350 in September, 1782. £160 in October, 1782. £70 in February, 1783. £580 in May, 1783. £145 16s in October, 1783. And to Jersey de Lisle and Co. £380 14s in February, 1783. £204 in May, 1783.

Thus in February and May he paid over £1,230 to these two firms.

In 1795 the following payments were made by William Johns. In the first five months £1,653 in all to Carteret. In February, March and April, £1,298 in all to Lukis. In July £480 12s in all to Carteret. In October £336 on account to Carteret. Thus in ten months over £3,760.

John Langmaid and Co. paid to Carteret £262 10s in August, 1795. £367 10s in September, 1795.

Richard Rowett and Co. paid £248 to Lukis in June, 1795.

Rowett, Langmaid, Willcock junior and Co. paid £347 in October, 1795, to Carteret.

John Clements and Co. £309 in October, 1795, to Carteret.

Barrett Mark and Co: £322 in February, 1796, to Lukis; £189 in February, 1797, to Lukis; £247 in March, 1797, to Lukis; £103 10s in May, 1797, to Lukis. £217 in March, 1797, to Maingy; £370 in April, 1797, to Maingy; £141 10s in May, 1797, to Maingy; £235 in June, 1797, to Maingy. Thus Barrett Mark and Co. paid £1,503 in five months of 1797 to two Guernsey firms.

Next comes a set of payments by Quiller

and others, viz: by John Quiller and Co., £390 in August, 1797, to Maingy; £437 in September, 1797, to Maingy; £450 in October, 1797, to Maingy.

By Quiller, Barrett and Co., £300 in December, 1797, to Maingy; £150 in January, 1798, to Maingy.

By Quiller, Mark, Barrett and Co., £312 in January, 1798, to Lukis; £220 in January, 1798, to Lukis.

(Of these two last payments, the former was on the October bill, and the second – later in the month – on the November bill).

Quiller Mark and Co. paid £188 in February, 1801, to Hillary Bovcault.

Wm. Quiller and Co. paid £469 in January, 1801, to Hillary Bovcault; £45 in February, 1801, to Hillary Bovcault; £38 in March, 1801, to Hillary Bovcault; £119 in April, 1801, to Hillary Bovcault.

(The January payment was actually made in two instalments against two accounts).

Richard Rowett paid £247 early in August, 1798, to Maingy; £247 late in August, 1798, to Maingy; £306 in October, 1798, to Maingy; £220 in November, 1798, to Maingy.

Thus Rowett paid £1,020 in four – or less than five – months: and, as the November payment was against a bill of 30th August, we again have a measure of the length of credit given.

I did not extract any examples from Robert Rean's many accounts of earlier date: but in 1800 he paid Maingy £400 in March, £440 in July and £400 in September.

It may naturally be asked how Job remitted all these credits to his clients in Guernsey: for it need scarcely be said that he did not ship some thousands of pounds annually in coins and bank notes. It is true that on various occasions he sent – certainly to Maingy, if not to others also – comparatively small sums by one or another of the smugglers, sometimes specifying so many of each of such and such coins in the currencies of several nations: but these consignments of coins may have been needed for special purposes, or possibly were sometimes in liquidation of the balance of an account. Now and then one of these Guernsey people turned up at Polperro or in the neighbourhood, and took some payment in cash from Job. Thus in 1778 Job paid fifty guineas to "Mr de Lisle at Polperro" and in 1792 three Maingys were in Looe and Polperro and St. Austell and took payment from Job. It looks too as though Mourant and Combes were paid personally in 1778 and 1779. For the most part, however, Job remitted to bankers or agents – in London, as I suppose, and as some certainly were: though how credits on a London bank enabled Guernsey dealers to buy goods to France during the long years of war between England and France is a question that might suggest some research into international finances at this period. Here are some examples.

Credits to account of	*Remitted to*
Hillary Bovcault & Co.	Samuel Dobree
John Lukis	Perchard & Co.
John Lukis	Brock and Lemesurier
Jersey and de Lisle	Lemesurier & Co.
Priaulx	Lemesurier & Co.
Maingy	Brock and Lemesurier

Maingy	Peter Perchard
Maingy	Dobree & Aubin
Maingy	Peter Maingy at
	St. Austell.

As I have mentioned in an earlier section, Job at first charged his Jersey clients a commission of half of one per cent on moneys paid in to their account: but already in 1782 and 1783 he was charging one per cent. Thus during thirty years his annual commission averaged only about fifty guineas. No wonder he charged them postage in addition.

* * * * *

In working through these records of thirty years one is astounded by the apparent impunity and unconcern with which the smugglers and their financial confederates pursued their work, and by the implicit imbecile supineness of the Government. One tends indeed to feel supreme contempt for the Government in all this sphere. First it caused Parliament to enact and maintain laws of such character as to prompt the well known comment that trade would have ceased to exist but for the smugglers: and then, although smuggling was a capital offence, the Government seems – if we just follow this Polperro evidence – to have tamely submitted to having the law treated with utter derision. On the one hand, one asks whether two or three preventive cutters stationed at Guernsey should not have sufficed to prevent any cargoes of contraband from leaving the island, thus nipping the trade in the bud. On the other hand, since it must have been notorious to everyone that Job was regularly receiving large sums to the credits of the Guernsey dealers, and very obviously making regular use of H.M. postal service in connection with the smuggling business; and since, no doubt, this sort of thing was going on all along the south coast; could not the Government have taken powers from Parliament – if indeed it did not already possess such – to issue search warrants, to carry off all relevant books and papers, to attach moneys due to the dealers who supplied the smugglers, and to prosecute all bankers and agents concerned for conspiracy to evade the law. It is foolish and wrong to enact any law that, for whatever reason, cannot be enforced: but it is doubly foolish and wrong to enact bad or foolish laws, and then to allow them to be treated with general derision and systematically broken with general impunity. No doubt some individuals were caught, and paid the penalty. In May, 1782, Job debited Jersey and de Lisle with £7 12s "to my attendance on Brown's Tryal at Guild Hall Lond. And Expce for --?" I know no more about this case, and have no note of any second such. Since "Brown" is not a general local name; and since Jersey and de Lisle were debited; it is possible that Brown was an actual employee of theirs who had somehow fallen into the clutches of the law. No one however can work through Job's day books and ledgers without forming the impression that up to some years after 1800 the smugglers did just what they liked without the least apparent fear of any interference. They seem to have landed their cargoes of contraband as regularly and systematically, and with as much nonchalance, as though these had been cargoes of pilchards or coals.

Such then remained the state of affairs until about 1806: but not later than 1807 something must have happened that put an almost abrupt and dramatic stop to smuggling in Polperro – unless indeed one choose to assume that smuggling went on as before but that Job almost suddenly ceased to function as the smugglers' banker. This alternative supposition seems improbable: the business – as may have been observed – had declined very much in 1806: and it will be shown that Job was in touch with several of the Guernsey firms some years later. I provisionally infer therefore that the imbecile authorities woke up at long last, and took measures that finally stopped smuggling on the old scale. As I have said, the figures had fallen low in 1806 and 1807: and in 1808 nothing seems to have been brought over but a pipe of port wine for Job at £40 7s. The next entry that I found is one of January, 1812, debiting Maingy with the expense of a messenger to P. Maingy at St. Austell: but the amount of the debit had not been filled in. Then we come to 1815, when there is an account of only £142 13s with Joseph de Jersey & Co from Barrett and Hicks and Rean. In daybook No. 29 there is almost no entry of 1815 and 1816 that could possibly refer to smuggling: but in December 1816, there is a note about "Peter Maingy Esq. of Roscoff". Thus it would appear that Maingy lost little time after the end of the long war between England and France in establishing himself on the Breton coast. In 1820 Benjamin Rowett went to Roscoff at Maingy's charges – presumably to assist in concocting some smuggling rascality. These odd entries and one to follow prove that Job kept in touch with at least three Guernsey firms, and certainly tend to discount any conjecture that smuggling went on after 1807 as before but that Job had ceased to have anything to do with it. It is amusing to notice that, after the credit to Lukis in 1808 for Job's port, there is no entry to his credit until 1819 when the overseers of Lansallos remitted £25 10s for the expenses of a pauper in Guernsey – obviously a Lansallos parishioner who had drifted thither. The remittance was repeated in 1820.

Now against my suggestion that Polperro smuggling was somehow stopped about 1807 it may be objected that Couch (on p. 85 of his "History of Polperro") records the death in 1810 of the smuggler Robert Mark whose notable epitaph may be read on a stone now placed in Talland church adjacent to the South door. Couch's date is, however, a blunder or misprint: for the date on the stone is 1802. Probably it is not generally known that Mark's wonderful epitaph was plagiarized verbatim – unless it was a stock epitaph in times of violence – from one in Lansallos churchyard (on the left of the path from the gate to the South door of the church) to the memory of John Perry, who was similarly killed by a cannonball in 1779.

On p. 98 of Couch's History is a statement that probably explains the sudden apparent extinction of smuggling in Polperro. He says that "at the beginning of the present (ie. nineteenth) century smuggling was carried out so daringly and to such an extent as to call for better organized means to repress it. Captures were frequent: and the law was rigorously enforced on all offenders ….. A boat and crew were stationed at Polperro: and this, I have been told, was the germ of the Preventive or Coastguard service …. This Polperro preventive boat was the first in Cornwall and, it is said, in England". Now it appears to me probable that this Preventive station was established here in 1807 or 1808.

*   *   *   *

It seemed desirable to carry on the story without a break from the days when Polperro paid the Guernsey dealers thousands of pounds annually to practically the close of Job's records:

but now we must revert to those palmy days of smuggling, when we find such a wonderful array of names of those paying in to the accounts of the Guernsey firms that there is much temptation to surmise that nearly every family in Polperro was engaged in smuggling. On one page of the ledger account with Hillary Bovcault & Co for January and February 1800, I found payments from Bartlett, Broughton (a new and unfamiliar name), Bunt, Coath, Forward, Fowler, Hicks, Johns, Langmaid, Libby, Lightfoot, Minards, Pearce, Roose, Rowe, Rowett, Swartman, Toms and Wills: yet so far from being really representative was this page that no payments from Barrett, Bowden, Mark, Quiller or Rean, for instance, happened to occur on it. I cannot guess what percentage of Polperro names one might collect from some dozens of such ledger pages of various years: but I took just this one sample. I found even Zebedee Minards the fisherman making various payments to Lukis – though I rather think only for small items. One very striking feature in any such list of smugglers is that we find so many names familiar to us as the names of farming families, e.g. Coath, Hutton, Langmaid, Rean, Rowe and – perhaps significantly – Roose. As I suggested, when discussing the derivation of fishermen from farming families, it seems very possible that some farmers' sons passed from farming to fishing via smuggling.

I was amused to find that on occasions the Guernsey firms stood treat to the smugglers: and I have noted the following entries regarding such treats. At Christmas, 1796, Job debited Lukis three guineas for a treat to Charles Rowett and Co., and at Christmas, 1797, one guinea for a treat to the same, and half a guinea for a treat to John Rowett and Co. Moreover also at Christmas, 1797, Maingys were debited one guinea for a treat to Charles

Rowett and Co. – who thus fared pretty well! – and one guinea for a treat to Charles Hutton and Co. In October, 1799, Maingys were debited "to Wm. Minards and Co. £2 2s 0d for a treat by order N. Maingy": and in March, 1800, there was a debit against Maingys – "to all your dealers a treat at Christmas £10 4s 6d". I do not know whether such dealers on a large and lordly scale as Barrett and Mark and Quiller and Richard Rowett condescended to share in this treat or not. In July, 1802, Job debited Maingys – "To John Rowett & Co. Expce at the New Inn on paying a bill the 12 October last 5/-"; and – "To do. For a dinner to themselves and Ship's Company 26th February last £9 18s 6d". There was also the debit – "To the Unity's Company £4 9s 10d". Couch tells us in his History of Polperro that "the Unity is stated to have made five hundred successful trips …. without having met with a single serious misadventure".

* * * *

I noted that Job's Guernsey clients must have sent him now and again commissions on account of their private kitchens presumably: for he occasionally consigned turkeys, legs of mutton and beef to them. Reciprocally he got from them his port wine and spirits.

* * * *

In conclusion I must add the reminder that the neighbouring gentry seem to have had no objection whatever to defrauding the revenue and abetting law-breakers by buying direct from these smugglers. For instance, that pillar of State and Church, the reverend Sir Harry Trelawny Bart., undoubtedly a J.P. for the county, paid

John Quiller £10 in 1777 for spirits at various times, and £8 8s in 1799 for spirits and liquor during that year. Similarly too Captain Eastcott bought direct from the smugglers.

PRIVATEERING FROM POLPERRO

Perhaps it is not generally realised that during certain periods privateering was as characteristic an industry of the Polperro people as was smuggling: but emphatically it was. The accounts and general business connected therewith entailed an enormous amount of work on Job: for he was definitely the privateers' banker and general man of business. When a vessel was being fitted out or repaired; when stores and weapons were shipped; when commissions – ie. letter of marque authorizing the capture of enemy vessels – had to be obtained; and when all sorts of other expenses had to be met; Job paid the charges and debited the owners of the vessel. When prizes had been captured, it was necessary that they should be legally condemned in a prize-court: and Job paid all the fees. On the other hand, when prizes and their cargo were sold, Job received the proceeds: and then in due course he shared out the balance of credit over debit. So far as I can judge from his account books alone I should say that privateering gave him proportionately far more work than did smuggling: but whether this inference would be confirmed by an examination of his correspondence we do not know.

In dealing with my notes and extracts on privateering it will be best to follow a chronological order pretty closely. Let it be remembered that

England was at war with the American Colonies – now the United States – from July, 1774, to November, 1782; with France from February, 1778, and with Spain from April, 1780, to January, 1783; and with Holland from December, 1780, to September, 1783. Then followed a peace lasting over nine years, during which there could, of course, be no privateering. Couch says in his "History of Polperro" (p.88) that "in time of war the occupation of of smuggling was exchanged for that of privateering": but the records quoted in the preceding section prove that smuggling went on vigorously during the long years of war.

Now although war with America had begun in 1774, and with France early in 1778, I have found nothing about privateering in Job's accounts earlier than 1781. It is true that the earliest daybook, No. 26 in the catalogue, carries us back only to 1782: but the first ledger, No. 34, was begun in 1778. Moreover the story told by Couch (pp. 89-90) of Job's success in reclaiming for the Polperro privateers a prize which they had captured from the French at the very outbreak of war – although they had a commission against the Americans only – proves that Polperro men must have been engaged in privateering at least as early as 1777. Couch says, that, when this privateer was fitted out, Job was appointed to keep the accounts; and that the £500 given to him from the proceeds of the reclaimed prize laid the foundation of his fortunes. This statement certainly tallies with the facts that Job must have been struggling to make a living as schoolmaster at least as late as the end of 1775 – witness John Clements' exercise-book! – that his earliest ledger extant dates from 1778, and that none of his trading ventures can be traced back to an earlier date than 1784 – as an inspection of the catalogue will show. It seemed desirable to prefix these explanations to the extracts from his books about privateering.

In 1781 six and a half pages of the ledger (No. 34) are occupied by between 200 and 250 entries of "Disbursements on the Swallow Letter of Marque". The total sum exceeds £1,500 and includes payments for food, arms, work on the vessel, "4 Commissions" at £17 each, and £460 to "Manoel Ferdinandis for Detention of his Ship and Demurrage". It is obvious that the Swallow had captured a vessel which was not a lawful prize – and the name of the owner suggests the possibility that the vessel may have been Portuguese instead of Spanish. The owners of the Swallow must have made very wry faces at the payment of £460 compensation for their little mistake. Seeing that privateering was not much better than legalised and limited piracy, and that those engaged in the work were probably too often a pretty rough – not to say ruffianly – set of men it is satisfactory to find that the Government kept a tight hand on them by requiring the legal condemnation of each prize, and by enforcing the restitution of any vessel unlawfully taken and compensation to the foreign owner.

The four Commissions mentioned were the letters of Marque authorising the capture of American, Dutch, French and Spanish ships respectively: and an entry in a later year proves definitely that they were such and were not commissions to the officers of the Swallow.

There are also pages of disbursements in January and February, 1781, on the Good Intent – the total amounting to £839: while from March of this year to February, 1783, there were payments totalling £62 – leaving a balance of £68 13s 2d due to the owners. So far then this does not seem to have been eminently profitable work. Elsewhere Job debited the Good Intent's account with only three guineas for his "trouble 10 days settling the Demurrage on the Schooner". Had the Good Intent also made an unlawful capture: or should the entry have been against the Swallow as aforesaid?

We have some account of the arms provided for these two vessels early in 1781, namely for the Swallow

12 guns and Shott - £60 3s.
12 carriages and blocks etc. - £23 14s

And for the Good Intent
12 guns and Shott - £58 17s 8d
Carriages, worms, etc. for ditto - £28 9s 4d.

Of course, to us nowadays it seems ludicrous and almost incredible that the actual cannons cost less than five pounds each. For the rest – cutlasses cost 4s and 3s each, hammocks 3s 6d each, gunpowder 7½d and 8d per pound, and a four-oared boat £10 3s 6d. As the Good Intent's equipment included "30 Handcoffs" at 1s 1d each, one realises that no risks were taken of a mutiny by any of the prisoners.

In the daybook No. 26 there are numbers of entries to the account with the Swallow's owners: and these include constant debits for work done on the vessel and materials supplied: and there are endless payments of prizemoney. One quickly learns to regard the owners of the Swallow as synonymous with John Quiller and Co.: but there is clear evidence that, whether included in the "and Co." or not, Jersey and de Lisle of Guernsey had shares in the venture. On 7th August, 1782, Job credited the Swallow with cash received from Edward Richards and Co., for "Goods sold them two voyages the men's being included £393 4s 10d". On 10th August there is an entry – "Paid the men for their Goods £62 12s 10d". I suppose that the reference is to a sale of privateering loot and not to an interlude of smuggling. It is, however, curious that in October, 1782, three Commissions for the Swallow were taken out at £17 each, no doubt against France and Holland and Spain. I do not know whether such letters of marque were issued for a definite limited period only, or why those issued early in 1781 were no longer valid. Had the Swallow been out of commission for a time: and, if so, were the goods sold to Richards smuggles after all?

There is one entry – about which I should like a good deal more information – detailing "disbursements on the Swallow when seized by Captain Payton".* The seizure occurred in or before April, 1783: and the account ran on to May, 1784. The total expenses seem to have been £351 6s: and these were debited in proportions, not all the same, against the vessel, J. Quiller and Co., May, Hockins, Lukey and Tinney. Now, in the first place we must suppose that the Swallow had been concerned in or suspected of some irregularity or illegality, and had consequently been seized by the commander of a warship: and it may be significant that peace had been made with France and Spain in January, 1783. In the second place it is clear that four Polperro people besides Quiller and Co. were

---

* The *Swallow*, commanded by William Johns and loaded with a contraband cargo of tea and gin worth £2,000,was seized by HMS *Beaver* (Captain Joseph Peyton) off Lundy Island in April 1783.

at this time sharers in the Swallow: but why was one proportion – the same as Quiller's – charged against the vessel herself? In the third place it is interesting to find that all the partners other than Quiller seem to have been landsmen: for Hockins and May were presumably farmers and Lukey the grocer; while the name Tinney I have found nowhere else except as that of the carpenters working for Talland parish in the second quarter of the century. I was particularly interested therefore to find Tinney's name here. One does not know whether Jersey and de Lisle were no longer shareholders: and John Baker's name does not appear on the list of contributors, although he had shares in the Swallow and perhaps in the Good Intent also.

Job went to London on business connected with the seizure of the vessel: but in 1783 he debited the Swallow's account with £15 14s 5d also "to Expce in London 5 weeks with the arbitrators on the Rusee" – one of the prizes.* On closing the account at the end of 1784 he charged only one guinea "to writing an in finite number of letters". Job certainly seems to have undercharged his clients.

One might well be curious to know how many men one of these Polperro privateers carried: and by good luck, I found in No. 34 a list which I now subjoin.

---

* The *La Rusee* was a French merchantman captured by the *Swallow* in 1781 off Spain. The two vessels were subsequently seized by a Liverpool privateer, the *Harlequin*. Job spent several months securing the release of both after a lengthy legal battle.

"A List of the Crew on Board the Good Intent Letter of Marque when she Captured the Prize Snell Jager."

Sharrock Jenkins, Commander, 140 shares
Charles Polgrain, Master

Francis Johns, Mate	Henry Tapril
William Cock, Lieut.	Richard Barrett
Joseph Bowden, Do.	John May
Michael Jenkings, Do.	Richard Naptune
Joseph Polgrain, Seaman	Charles Dun
William Venton	James Vigus
Joseph Pearce	John Allen
Arthur James	James Ball
Richard Stephings	John Forward
James Turner	Matthew Jenkings
George Rowe	William Rean
Stephen Hoil	Bartholomew Warren
William Jenkings	Nicholas Jenkings
William Greet	William Forward
Alexander Harris	Nicholas Johns
John Sawle	John Jasper
Ed. Snell	William Jasper
Attey Marting	William Searle
James Robins	Richard Perry
Alexander Peters	William Langmaid
John Andrew	John Mark
Richard Peters	John Jenkings
Michael Dillon	Henry Hoyton
Richard Forward	John Peters
John Potter	John Gill
William Griffiths	John Mills
John Batting	Richard Ball
Silvester Minards	John Pascho
Henry Jenkings	Job Jenkings
Reginald Langmaid	Archelas Jenkings
John Pascho jr.	Richard Jennings jr.

Thus a Polperro lugger – or luggar, as Job always wrote it – carried a total complement of 64, who must have been packed like sardines until the crowd was diminished by drafting off prize crews into captured vessels.

Some of the names are not local – so far as Talland and Lansallos records and general knowledge can be relied on. Jenkings was a surprise to begin with: but a ledger account of Job's with "Sharrock Jenkings of St. Mawes" disposes of him and presumably of the seven other Jenkings, Cock, Robins, Dillon, Potter. Griffiths, Naptune (?), Vigus and Mills, I assume to have been strangers – possibly picked up by Jenkings at Falmouth. Hoil is presumably one more variant of Hole: and Batting and Marting were obviously Batten and Martin. I was astonished by the number of landsmen's names: and their presence once more suggests the obvious possibility that through privateering as through smuggling farmers' sons may have eventually drifted into fishing in later life.

Of those assumed to be imported strangers William Griffiths may well have been father of, or kin to, the Richard Griffith on the 1808-9 list of Polperro boatmen: and one would greatly like to know the connection between John Potter and the Tom Potter whose history is told on pp 85-88 of Couch's book. One can quite understand that men recruited from other ports for a Polperro privateer may later have married Polperro girls and settled here.

To revert to the list – there is a note that the prize Snell Jager from Cadiz to Ostend was taken in partnership with the Garland (Captain Gambrell) from Plymouth: and we may now pass on to consider what is said about the values of the prizes taken by the Swallow and the Good Intent. The Swallow's prize La Rusee apparently brought in £1,733 19s 3d for sharing out – ie. as nett proceeds after the payment of all fees, etc.

It looks as though even this large sum was brought in by the sale of the vessel only: for another entry credits the account with £4,890 15s 10d – less however, I think, the heavy charges to be mentioned later. Now this second credit represented, I suppose, the sale of the cargo: and, as there are special entries about the value of the "cabin", I infer that this included some special loot. As we have seen, there was a lengthy business of arbitration about this vessel or her cargo.

The San Luis de Bilbo and cargo seem to have been sold for £482 of which £375 seems to have been nett balance available for distribution: while the St. Anne Doré was sold for £130, and the wine in her for nearly £129 – at Guernsey.

The Sarge Clixer, or Clixis, was evidently loaded with "rozin". The duties paid on this to the collector at Looe, when it was landed there, amounted to £182 3s 6d: and the resin seems to have been sold for £554 7s. The prize Le Chardon seems to have been sold for only £63: but the Head Money on the sixteen men in her eventually brought in £80. This we learn that the Government paid £5 for each prisoner brought in by these licensed corsairs: and one cannot help wondering whether such payments may originally have been instituted partly at least as a bribe to induce privateering crews to bring in their prisoners instead of finding some excuse for killing or drowning many of them. Why there was a delay of over two years and a half in paying the head money on the prisoners from Le Chardon is a question to be left unanswered.

Now let us take note of some of the expenses incurred on the capture of each prize. The following were the proctor's charges or fees "on condemning" the prizes: and I infer that these "proctors" were either officials of the prize court, or, in effect, advocates or attorneys whom it was essential to employ.

1781 – On the Joachim Marie, £37 4s

1782 – On the Le Chardon, £36 9s

1782 – On the St. Anne Dorée, £30 14s

1783 – On the St. Luis de Bilbo, £28 10s 7d or £25 7s 7d

1783 – On the Sarge Clixer or Clixis, £22 3s 7d or £25 6s 7d in another entry.

1783 – On the La Rusee, £84 14s 3d

In addition there were sometimes, if not always, other charges and expenses. For instance, it cost £17 4s to take depositions about the S. Anne Dorée and £11 13s for depositions on Le Chardon: while the total expenses on the latter were a little over £60. Again, the actuary's bill on the Sarge Clixer was £17 9s 6d, and on the St. Luis de Bilbo £18 6s 1d. I do not know whether an actuary's services were alternative to depositions: but I found no mention of the latter when there was an actuary's bill. The arbitrator's and actuary's charges on La Rusee accounted for £36: William de Jersey on London, managed to disburse £331 9s 8d over this valuable prize: and there were other expenses. Job wrote de Jersey a letter of protest against his tremendous bill. Altogether there seems to have been many pickings for those who incurred no risks of any sort and endured no hardships.

When peace was signed with Holland – the last remaining enemy – in September, 1783, privateering came to an end for the time: but one may suspect that the vessels and many of the men, no longer needed for this work, were not left idle but became available for smuggling. Late in

October, 1786, Job sold to Quiller and Johns "my ¼ Proportion in the Luggars Swallow and Brilliant" for £197 10s. This entry seems to contradict Couch's statement on p. 90 of his "History of Polperro" that, except in the first venture which brought him the five hundred pounds, Job "had no share in the risks or profits of privateering" – unless we choose to assume that he had not bought shares in these luggers until after September, 1783.

In February, 1793, war with France broke out again: and privateering was promptly resumed by the Polperro men. It is suggestive and interesting to find that Maingy – the Guernsey dealer who sold so largely to the Polperro smugglers – had shares in two or three of the Polperro privateers, just as de Jersey and de Lisle had shares in the Swallow a dozen or so years earlier. During 1793 Job debited Maingy to cost on ½ in Lively Privateer £164 14s 9d and £25 8s 5d on the first cruise, and £77 2s 5d on the second; and to cost on the Sedwell Privateer £21 5s; and to sundries for the Brilliant Luggar – also a privateer - £79 10s 7d. In August he credited Maingy –

> Your bill on the Lively Privateer
> 1st Cruise - £88 9s 6d
> 2nd cruise - £209 19s 2d

Thus Maingy evidently sold supplies of some sort to the Lively to such an extent that his receipts for these exceeded his share of the outlay.

The following entry in daybook No. 27 is too puzzling for any certain interpretation. "Received of Mr Job thirty-five Pounds for 1/32 in the Sedwell Privateer bought of Fras. Stocker of Fowey with the earnings belonging to said share since her first going to sea. Robert Rean, 5 June, 1783." Whether

Rean had bought from Stocker and then sold to Job, or whether he simply acted as agent for Stocker in selling to Job I will not undertake to decide: but in either case we seem again to find Job buying a share in a privateer. According to this reckoning the Sedwell was valued at £1,120; but during the year she was sold for £700, of which 1/16 went to Maingy. During the same year the Lively was sold for £1,100, of which 1/16 went to Quiller; and Maingy bought the Lively's prize Eulalie for £510 – of which, however, something remains to be said later.

There is also the following entry, which once more exhibits Job as a shareholder in a privateer – in spite of Couch's averment to the contrary. "It is hereby agreed between Mr John Quiller and Sons and Z. Job that the 1/8 reserved in the Brilliant Luggar Privateer shall be divided into five parts the 20th November, 1793.

Z. Job

Richard Quiller."

In different ink there is the addition "4 parts for Mr Quiller and Sons, one part for Z. Job". It may be noticed that Richard Quiller signed – his father being no penman. I was interested to notice that, whereas during the former war the vessels had been described as the Swallow e.g. Letter of Marque, they were now always designated privateers. However I found in the heading of one ledger page of 1782 that the Swallow was called a privateer.

In 1795 there occurs the following entry in daybook No. 27. "March 30. Mr John Quiller and Sons hath sold and Zephaniah Job hath purchased 1-16th of the Three Brothers Luggar at the price of twelve hundred pounds for the whole which 1-16th Proportion I promise to pay them on demand.

Witness my hand
Zephaniah Job
Richard Quiller
William Quiller."

I will not undertake to say whether at this time the Three Brothers was commissioned as a privateer or was engaged in trade. I should have inclined strongly to the former alternative but for the fact that the earlier vessel of the same name, lost in 1794 as previously noted, was apparently a trader. In 1797 a share of 1-16th in the Three Brothers was again sold for £75 – ie. at the same price as in 1795.

In April, 1796, Job – clearing up old accounts, I suppose – credited Maingy with ¼ of £300 14s 10d as owners' proportion of the Lively's prize Eulalie – which Maingy had bought for £510 in 1793 – and "¼" but really barely 1-6th of £69 2s 1d on the prize La Clubb and 1-16th of owners' proportion of a prize to the Sedwell at £53 7s 1d. Per contra he debited Maingy with ¼ and 1-16th of the expenses of the Lively and Sedwell respectively. Now does the difference between £510 and £300 14s 10d on the value of the Eulalie mean that the owners took three-fifths and the crew two-fifths? The emphasis on the owners' proportion seems to justify such an inference.

In May, 1797, Job sold his 1/8 share in the lugger Brilliant to Maingy for £5 16s 3d – an unintelligibly low price if this was a genuine deal and not a mere cover for some other transaction. It does not certainly follow that this was the same Brilliant in which ¼ share had been sold in 1786: for I believe that the name was given to more than one vessel. Yet once again, however, we find evidence pointing to Job's actual partnership in a privateer. In August, 1798, John Quiller and Co.'s share for prize-money earned by the Brilliant was £179 10s 8d, besides £82 6s 8d to John Quiller junior; and again £178 10s 3d. I may once more remark that privateering involved a tremendous amount of book-keeping and accountancy and legal business; and that Job, as accountant and business manager, very emphatically had no sinecure.

The Peace of Amiens, signed in March, 1802, brought only a year's respite from war: and in 1803 the privateers were at work again. I have however hardly any notes about them after this date: and it is possible that the apparent loss of a daybook between Nos. 28 and 29 may in some measure account for my lack of data. It is also, of course, possible that Job, for some reason, dropped a good deal of the privateering business; though I have no actual proof that he did.

In the summer and autumn of 1803 there are many entries in No. 30 of debits to the account of the privateer cutter Industry. A bill of sale to Job was drawn – possibly as security for the expenses that he was to meet. John Quiller had 1-10th share in her. The "French and Dutch Commissions" – ie. letters of marque authorising the capture of French and Dutch vessels – cost £22 4s each now; and the "Protection" £1 5s. This "Protection" was a certificate that safeguarded the holder from seizure by a press-gang. Naturally among the entries of the earlier period there were references to such "Protections", although I have not actually extracted a note of any example but this one. In November, 1803, there is an entry that the judge's certificate of condemnation of the brig Despatch cost £4 4s. As this fee was absurdly lower than the proctors' charges of twenty years earlier, one would like to know whether the prize-courts had been remodelled and proctors' charges abolished, or not. It looks as though the brig was sold for £250. The name is a mystery; for we were not then at war with America: yet how came a French or Dutch vessel to have such a name?

In 1807 Phillis and Wills were debited in connection with the privateer Unity – which was, I suppose, the famous smuggling vessel. It is notable that the entries about the Industry and the Unity are in "subsidiary" daybooks – as I described them in the Catalogue. I incline to interpret such relegation of the entries to these subsidiary daybooks as indicating that the business was of less importance to Job than of old, and anyhow did not involve ledger accounts as originally. I am rather struck by the fact that there is nothing in my privateering notes about the privateer John Bull, which is mentioned in the harbour accounts as having been fitted out in 1805: and I have nothing later than the reference to the Unity in 1807. That privateering continued, and that Polperro men were engaged in it later than 1807, is proved by an entry that I found some years ago in the Lansallos registers recording the marriage of William Quiller – son of one of the three brothers and grandson of the notable John – commander of the privateer Pheasant, to Ann Rowett in 1811. It is curious, by the way, that these people gave their semi-piratical vessels such names as Swallow and Pheasant and Good Intent; whereas Hawk and Vulture and Evil Omen would have been more appropriate.

Perhaps as a pendent to this section I may quote without comment a passage which I found in a current journal while I was working at Job's books. "'The conduct of all privateers' – said Lord Nelson in 1804 – 'is, so far as I have seen, so near piracy, that I wonder any civilized nation can allow them.' That, unfortunately, was the view of most naval officers. When the Navy was efficient, the privateers were not needed: and when the Navy failed . . . . the privateers saved them situation; and the Navy disliked them accordingly: for . . . . there was always the question of prize-money."

THE PROFITS FROM SMUGGLING AND PRIVATEERING.

One would very much like to know what profits were made by smuggling and privateering, ie. what average income over a series of years: but this is a desire that must remain unsatisfied. If all those engaged in these occupations had kept banking accounts with Job, and had paid in all their takings, then, by deducting their outlays, we could of course reach the desired result: but actually only two or three seem to have kept banking accounts. I can say nothing about such smugglers on a large scale as Barrett and Mark and Rean, for examples, and naturally nothing about the numbers who seemed to have smuggled on a small scale. I have notes on the accounts of three men: but these tell us more about privateering than smuggling.

In October 1783 William Johns was credited with over £704 from privateering, but debited with nearly £33 as his share of a loss on the Swallow. This seems to represent the prize gains on two years' privateering: and nearly £630 of it came from that rich prize La Rusee. On the other hand, what had been Johns' share of the cost of fitting the Swallow and meeting current expenses: and must such outlay be deducted from about £670 now received? John Baker seems to have made about £600 during the same period: but one cannot tell from the entries whether nearly all, or less than two-thirds, represented privateering gains. However, Baker must have been a good deal wealthier than this ledger account would suggest: for in May, 1786, he lent Sir Harry Trelawny £2,000 on a mortgage, though borrowing £500 of this from Job on a note of hand. I suspect that smuggling and privateering may have been only extras – so to say – with Baker.

John Quiller was, from our point of view, a far more satisfactory client of Job's; and most of my information on the present topic refers to him. An account of Job's, Quiller's and Johns' with William de Jersey of London from February, 1782, to April, 1784, amounted to over £1,500 – of which only £141 had been credited earlier than November, 1783. I think that this represented privateering profits, and that Johns' and Quiller's shares may likely enough have been transferred to their accounts with Job. Once more, too, we have what may well be evidence of Job's share in privateering ventures. John Quiller's account with Job in 1782 ran to about £338, and in 1783 to £1,174 – of which latter amount £998 came from La Rusee. In 1784 it reached practically £727 by the end of October: while from November to the end of May, 1785, there was an income of £717 which, however, included the repayment of £300 previously lent on interest. In 1784 Quiller received £500 on eleven "voyages" of the Brilliant, besides £129 on ¼ of the "gain" from the Brilliant – ie., as I suppose, on the owner's share. I thought at first that this represented smuggling profits: but on reflection I feel uncertain whether the payments may not have been for privateering successes by the Brilliant in preceding years – especially since the intervals between the captures of prizes and the actual distribution of the plunder to the beneficiaries seem to have been lengthy.

From May, 1785, to July, 1789, Quiller's account was £638 13s 8d: but nothing was paid in to his credit after April, 1786. In August, 1789, I found £149 paid in to his credit: and the account was continued into 1790, and finally reached £587. The account for 1792-93 reached nearly £1,455: but part of this came from the sale of a lugger: and there is another account for the same period amounting to only £1,376 and ending with a balance of £336 due to Quiller. The confusion seems to arise from some attempt to distinguish between Quiller personally and Quiller and Sons: and probably all was clear enough to Job and the Quillers. From 25th November, 1793, to January, 1797, there was an account with Quiller and Sons that ran to £861. Quiller owned in 1794 1/8 of the lugger Brilliant, which was then sold for £2,000; and took 1/8 of the "gain" of the sloop Three Brothers in 1795, and 1/16 of the Lively's prizes: and bore the same proportions of the expenses. Here, of course, was privateering again.

One way and another Quiller did so well that in 1796 or earlier he lent John Grigg £500, repaid in 1799; and in 1800 he lent Sir Harry £1,300 on his and Job's joint bond. Job had also been similarly linked with Grigg in the loan to him: for apparently Quiller deemed the security in sufficient unless Job became a party to the bond. Herein was certainly a striking testimonial to Job's financial reputation with his neighbours – but a poor compliment to the great landowner, e.g.

We may reasonably suspect that, of those who made money by smuggling and privateering, too many carelessly dissipated their gains: but it seems pretty clear that Quiller was longheaded and thrifty. As regards the proceeds of smuggling one would very greatly like to know whether the bulk of the profits made remained with the smugglers – who took the risks including the risk of their lives – or whether they sold the goods at comparatively low prices to middlemen who made fortunes without enduring hardships or taking risks. If the smugglers were clever enough to secure the lion's share for themselves and to leave the middlemen only a reasonable commission – which I very much doubt – they were far luckier than their law abiding successors of today, the fishermen, who, in common with farmers and market gardeners, are shamelessly exploited by those non-producing middlemen who seize all the lion 's share for themselves. Whatever may have been the case with the smugglers, however, the privateers seem to have done fairly well.

THE PACKET OF DEEDS.

I mentioned at the end of the catalogue that there was a packet of so far unexamined deeds which I hoped to look through in due course. After writing all the foregoing and also the section that follows this I tackled this residue. In the packet were sundry accounts and receipted bills and several letters and other papers that need not detain us, two other documents to be described anon, over a dozen indentures of lease and mortgage and assignation, and a Rental of the Manor of Lansallos for 1805. This last was by far the most important find: and it is to be regretted that I did not discover it when I found the Rentals of Raphiel, and so lost the opportunity of dealing with the two manors together. Fortunately, it is very brief: and I did not think that in this case the tabular form need be transcribed. The tenements are numbered on this Rental; and the details are as follow:

No. 1, late Calloway's Cot, leased to John Congdon at 11s 6d rent with heriot of 3s 6d on the lives of himself, 54, Mary his wife, 54, and Samuel their son, 15.

No. 2, blacksmith's shop, leased to the same at 9s rent and 3s 4d heriot, on the lives of John Congdon, 18, Mary Congdon, 21, and Grace Hele, 38.

No. 3, High Park, leased to Miss Eastcott at 6s 8d rent and 10s heriot, on the lives of her brother Thomas, 34, and William Powne 40.

No. 4, four houses and gardens in Lansallos churchtown, leased to Charles Guy at 19s 6d rent and 19s heriot on the lives of Susanna Mark, 38, Elizabeth Guy, 33, and Ann Quiller, 44.

No. 5, Clemence's Polventon, leased to Ralph Powne at 19s 6d rent and 7s 8d heriot on the lives of himself, 29, William Toms, 29, and Elizabeth Toms, 30.

No. 6, garden in Polruan, let to Richard Pryer at 6s rent and 2s 6d heriot, on the lives of himself, 74, his daughter Ann, 44, and his daughter Temperance, 41.

No. 7, Styart's house, meadow and orchard, leased to John Pearse at 6s 6d rent and 10s heriot on the lives of William Powne 40, Mary Pearse, 23, and Samuel Pearse, 11.

No. 8, Tregavithick, leased to Robert Rean at £1 11s 2d rent (but no heriot entered) on the lives of himself, 51, and his wife Ann (whose age is not entered).

No. 9, East and West Polgassick, leased to (the executors of) Richard Rowett at £2 4s 2d rent and £5 5s heriot on the lives of Ann Rowett, 58, Richard Rowett, 36, and William Rowett deceased, but 33 in 1805.

No. 10, late Bastard's at Polruan, leased to James Truscott in place of William Whipple, 47, Jenefer Bastard Whipple, 25, John Whipple, 19.

No. 11, Old Walls and a garden at Polruan, leased to William Pearse in place of William Whipple at 2s rent and 2s 6d heriot on the lives of lessee, 52, his son William, 23, and William Hicks, 24 (owing to the alterations one cannot determine whether these were Whipple lives on No. 11 or Pearse lives).

The only rack rent is that on the Barton of Lansallos and Coombe, leased to Thomas Rowe at £144.

There is the following endorsement on the Rental: "Chief Rent payable out of Polgassick.

To Lord Camelford..........	4	6
To Philip Rashleigh, Esq...	4	6
To Mr Millett.................	7	6
To Mr Hearle.................	3	8
	1 0	2
Gift to the poor of Lansallos	1 0	0
Out of Coombe Estate to Mr John Honey	1	0

Allowed Mrs Rowett out of the Convy. rent of Polgassick.

Z. Job."

Why a chief rent, ie., a ground rent should have been payable for parts of a manor, I do not understand.

Three entries in the Rental require brief comment. As I mentioned in the "Pedigrees of Polperro", the ancestor of the present Congdon family is reported to have migrated from Polkerris to Polperro about 130 years ago: and no kinship is known with the earlier Congdons of Lansallos or those of Talland. Now the tenant of Nos. 1 and 2 appears from the name of his son, Samuel, to have belonged to the Lansallos family of Congdons, and anyhow was not the Polkerris immigrant: yet he too was a smith, as was also the immigrant.

Secondly, the earliest tenant of No. 10, Bastard, bore the name of an eminent Devonshire family of landowners. Was he descended from some younger son, thus illustrating that fall through generations from great landlord to peasant of which I spoke in "The Records of Lansallos"?

Thirdly, it was astonishing to discover that Richard Rowett had held Polgassick farm. The number of Richard Rowetts is always bewildering: but I should be inclined to guess that this Richard was the great smuggler, and that he had taken to the land in middle life. Still the entry compels us to ask, however doubtfully, whether the Rowetts may have begun as a farming family and have taken to the water for smuggling and privateering. The farther one searches into these old records, the more amphibious one seems to find the population of Polperro.

*　*　*　*　*

There are five indentures of leases from the Manor of Raphiel, from which we can at least discover what amounts of "consideration" or fine was paid for the grant of a lease carrying a conventionary rent of only a few shillings. In 1775 a lease was granted to Thomas Toms, fisherman, on the lives of Mary Moore, Thomas Toms, aged 30, and Philippa, his wife. The consideration was thirty guineas and the surrender of a former lease; the rent 4s plus two lings or 2s; and the heriot 8s. The indenture is damaged, part on each side having decayed or been torn away. According to the names and ages of Toms and his wife, and the rent and heriots, this tenement would seem to have been No. 79: but damage to the indenture deprives us of the full description of the tenement.

In the same year a cottage and garden, lately held by Thomas Willcock, were leased to Thomas Bartlett on a fine of £65. The details as to the lives positively identify this as No. 21. Here again, the indenture is partly torn away.

In 1783 the "palaces" – ie. fish cellars – on the Tuner quay were leased to John Baker, in reversion of Elizabeth Lean, on the lives of himself aged 38 and his nephew Arthur Nicholls, aged about 3. The fine was £45; rent 2s and heriot 4s. This tenement must have been No. 4: but clearly Arthur Nicholls died before 1800; and Baker must have paid another fine for the addition of two young lives entered in the rental of 1800. This indenture is also partly torn away.

The three leases just described were granted by William and Jonathan Phillipps, but the next one was granted by Sir Jonathan Phillipps, and John Phillipps Carpenter. As may have been noted, these two families were curiously mixed up in the ownership of Raphiel and Lansallos: and the inference from the names is that a Carpenter had married a daughter of the Phillipps. Couch says that a moiety of the estate was given by Phillipps – whose name he doubly misspells – to Carpenter of Mount Tavy in Devon.

In 1794 a reversionary lease of No. 20 was granted to Eastcott for £6 6s. In effect this low charge was made apparently for the addition of his life to the two existing. The signature was witnessed by a John Eastcott, presumably an uncle or cousin.

In December, 1800, Hugh Fowler, fisherman, sold his lease of No. 22 – which we now learn had formerly been in the possession of William and Grace Jasper – to James Hill, yeoman, for £170. The price seems tremendous, as the only young life on the tenement was that of Hugh's son, John, now nearly or over 23. This is one of the tenements that could not be identified on the Rental of 1806: and we are no better off now as Hill does not appear in that rental as a tenant on lives. Incidentally I do not believe that Hugh Fowler would have made anything like enough as a fisherman to lease seven tenements of such value that he could sell the lease of one for £170. Perhaps "fisherman" was a pretty euphemism for smuggler.

The remaining indentures are a mixed bag: and I will catalogue them as briefly as possible. All the leases were on lives of course.

In 1751 Thomas Mayow of Bray leased part of a malt house in East Looe to Nicholas Harris. The indenture is so torn that full details cannot be determined: and there is an endorsement noting sale to William(?) Tucker(?).

In 1781 Thomas Mayow of Bray leased part Brent in Polperro to Ezekiel Rickard, fisherman, on the lives of his brother Richard, 35, John, 35, John Rickard, 7, and Ezekiel's daughter Jane, 7. The total fine was £53 16s; rent 5s, and dues and heriot 6s 8d. The dues, replaceable by money, were a capon at Christmas and two harvest journeys – ie. two days' work. And here, of course, we have a clear relic of ancient villain tenure. Rickards as carpenters are familiar: but I was astonished to find one a fisherman. Had he really prospered so by fishing; and, if so, what did he want with Lower Brent: or was "fisherman" only an euphemism here too? This indenture is partly faded from damp.

In 1773 John Buller leased to John Sargent a house and little meadow in Lansallos parish, apparently at Crumplehorn, formerly held by Charles Gilbert and later by John Avery. The fine was £9 9s; and the rent 4s. The ink of this indenture is much faded.

In 1776 William Toms, yeoman, assigned to Robert Keam, tinner (apparently), of St. Austell, a moiety of a tenement in Botallock, and his household goods and cattle and implements of husbandry. Toms' farm was on the Trelawny estate; and Keam's was one of the lives on which it was held.

At Midsummer, 1784, Job assigned to John Quiller two plots of garden ground on the Talland side of Polperro in exchange for five shillings and a garden plot and premises adjoining Job's house. Quiller was already building a house on the ground now assigned to him, the lease of which by Nicholas Kendall to Henry Johns and Richard Hobb had been recently purchased by Job from them. On the other hand Quiller had to purchase the lease for Job's life, in reversion of two existing lives, of the land that he was to give to Job. I suppose that on those manorial days freehold land could not be bought. It seems to me quite probable that the house which Quiller was building was that now known as "The Cottage" which has for long been in the possession of the Rowett family but was built by John Quiller.

In 1787 John Roskilly mortgaged his moiety of a tenement at Botallock in Boconnoc to William Hockin, alias Hocken, yeoman, of Lansallos, for £100. This was a Trelawny farm held on the lives of William A'Lee and Roskilly himself and his daughter Anne.

In 1794 R. Thomas assigned the lease of North Tregue to Courtis as aforesaid in an earlier section.

An indenture of 1880 is a conveyance by John Roskilly of Boconnoc, yeoman, and John Willcock junior, of Polperro, mariner, to James Roskilly, son of John. It seems that in 1798 John Roskilly mortgaged his farm to Thomas Perry of Polperro, "fisherman" – and pretty certainly smuggler! – who transferred the mortgage in 1799 to Willcock; and that now the younger Roskilly both repaid the mortgage and bought out his father's rights. The farm was Hill and the lease had been granted to John Roskilly's father in 1769 by the Hon. Thomas Pitt.

The last indenture is one of 1812 by which Charles Guy and his widowed sisters Elizabeth Rowett and Martha Rowett let Trenedon for fourteen years at a "clear rent" of £66 10s to William Gedye, of Lansallos, yeoman.

* * * * *

Only two other documents need mention. There is a copy of the probate, 1750, of the will 1745, and codicil, 1750, of Thomas Little, of Morval, clothier – the executors being his widow, Anne, and sons Denzil and Joseph. Under date 1771 there is an order of supersession of a commission in bankruptcy formerly granted against James Spershott, miller and corn factor, etc., of the Parish of Mortha, in Cornwall. Whether "Mortha" was a mistake for Morval, or whether Mortha in Talland parish was intended, must remain an open question.

THE LAST OF ZEPHANIAH JOB

As this story began with Zephaniah Job himself, so may it fitly end with him. It is to be regretted that we know nothing about Job's ancestry and, therefore, cannot opine whether in respect of his appreciable brain power and business capacity he was what naturalists call a sport, or whether there was some strain in his ancestry that would account for him and render the story of his rise from poverty to wealth less surprising. I imagine that Samuel Smiles of "Self Help" would have been highly delighted had he come across the history of Job and been enabled to quote it as exemplifying very successful self help.

In very occasional entries in Job's books there are references to several members of his family. First of all there is the following entry. "1779, August 17, Settled Acct. with Brother John Job for the Rent of Mingoes Comb Tenement and all the outgoings and club to Lady-day last," leaving "due to me £2 0s 4½d." There follow accounts ending 1789, of money lent, interest, nearly ten years' rent of Mingoes Comb at £2 10s yearly, and £7 7s "to pay the Supervisor at St. Agnes". The total is over

£82 with a per contra credit of £9 14s 3d, leaving a balance of £72 15s due to Zephaniah. I very greatly doubt whether he ever received payment of this balance. He appears to have employed this brother John on some business of his on at least one occasion. What has to be said presently tends to confirm my early inference that John was the father of Ananiah and Thomas – of whom in due course – but the question arises whether he was also the father of the younger Zephaniah, who, according to the entries in Nos. 41, 42 and 70, of the Raphiel Rental was born in 1769 or 1770. If so, John must certainly have been older than our Job who, according to the Raphiel entries, was only eighteen years older than his nephew Zephaniah junior, and was therefore born in 1751 or 1752. One the other hand, however, according to the age given on his tombstone, as quoted by Couch, Job must have been born in 1747: so a mistake was made, either in the Rental – ie., by Job himself! – or on the tombstone, or by Couch.*

In 1805 there is the entry – "advanced my nephew Zephaniah £5", and again in the same year there is an entry of £6 "for my nephew Zephaniah". From a tradition in the family it would seem that one of Job's nephews may have been more or less fitted to follow in his footsteps or at any rate assist him in his business, but died un timely: and I surmise that the younger Zephaniah was this nephew, and that "my nephew", who is occasionally mentioned in the ledger as Job's agent or representative in some business, was he. I surmise also that he may have been Job's destined heir and successor, and that, in such case, his death put an end to any

---

* The inscription on Job's headstone said that he died 'in the 75th year of his age'. He was, in fact, aged 73 at the time of his death.

plans that Job may have cherished of founding a business and banking family – he himself being a bachelor.

Occasionally in the daybooks there are entries of a few pounds to "sister Elizabeth" and "sister Sarah", both of whom – as will shortly appear – pre-deceased Job. It will be noted that Elizabeth married Tonkin and Sarah married Stevens.

On the last day of January, 1822, Job died. It is however a curious fact that we know nothing whatever of Job's doings after 6th October, 1820, when daybook No. 29 was completed, except that we can find from No. 31 that corn was bought as late as 7th February, 1821, while some entries in the fragmentary No. 25 seem to indicate that some business of different sorts was done in 1821. As there is no evidence whether a final daybook and final other books have been destroyed or lost, we cannot tell whether during the year and a quarter before his death Job was winding up his businesses and preparing to retire, or whether only the absence of books creates some illusion to this effect. It is curious that the endorsement by William Minard to No. 29 harmonized so aptly with my erroneous dating of Job's death.

Now the story of his death is that he ate a heavy meal at night and was found dead in bed the next morning. Strange to say, although he was such a model man of business, and had so much to do with making and executing other people's wills, no will of his own was to be found. The family tradition is that he had intended to make Sir Harry Trelawny his heir; but – as it was put – he died sooner than he intended to. That is an annoying sort of accident which has befallen many folk: but it is precisely because such unforeseen accidents are so apt to happen, and because any intentions of deferring death to a thoroughly convenient season are so futile, that prudent men make their wills betimes. However, as no will was to be found, letters of administration were granted to his nephews, Ananiah and Thomas Job – the latter described as yeoman – and the estate was divided among the next of kin. The value of the estate, and the debts and liabilities, were returned as follows:

	£	s	d
Cash in House......................	1,442	19	1
Plate, linen, china, pictures, etc..	228	12	3
Wearing apparel...................	25	0	0
Jewels, etc..........................	5	16	6
Wine and liquors.................	125	5	0
Horses..............................	61	0	0
Farming stock, etc................	398	10	3
Leasehold estates..................	2,138	12	6
£4,600 of 3 per cent at 80 7/8	3,645	10	0
£2,800 of 5 per cent Navy at 101 ⁵/₈	2,842	0	0
£4,000 of 3 per cent Navy at 80 ³/₈	3,193	17	6

	£	s	d
	£14,107	3	1

	£	s	d
Rents..............................	72	14	9
Dividends..........................	129	0	0
Cash for book and other debts..	3,986	14	0
Cash from ships..................	620	19	0
	£18,916	10	10
Deduct as below...................	£11,375	10	10
	£7,541	0	0
Administration Duty returned on account debts.....................	225	0	0
"Clear Residue"	£7,766	0	0

The expenses and liabilities which accounted for the enormous deduction of over £11,000 were as follows:

	£	s	d
Administration charges of obtaining (stamp only)......................	465	0	0
Funeral expenses.................	135	9	5
Expenses of executorship or administration....................	252	7	11
Debts on simple contract....... (including some expenses of administration)	£1,533	9	11
Debts on Bond, etc.............	£8,898	3	7
	£11,375	10	10

The "clear residue" of £7,766 was divided thus:

1/12th (ie. £647 3s 4d) to Ananiah Job

1/12th to Thomas Job

4/12ths to Elizabeth Prout "descendant" of Sarah Stevens sister of Z. Job

4/12ths to John Tonkin and Catherine Goyen (wife of Richard Goyen) "descendants" of Z. Job's sister, Elizabeth Tonkin.

1/12th to Richard Goyen "descendant" of Z. Job's brother.

From these data it seems clear that the division was "per stirpes" among the representatives of Job's brother and two sisters: but, as all three of these were dead, the division was legally bound to be "per capita". The only explanation that I can suggest of what would otherwise seem to be an insoluble puzzle is that one of these three had survived Job by however short a time – thereby reducing the shares of Ananiah and Thomas from over £1,100 at any rate to £647. Moreover it is clear that either Job had no other brother or sisters, or that any such had died and left no descendants.

Owing to the division of the estate "per stirpes" we learn that Ananiah and Thomas were brothers, and that a sister of theirs had married Goyen leaving only a son Richard who was married to his cousin Catherine Tonkin. (I am assuming that the "descendants" of the sisters were their children and not their grandchildren, and that Richard Goyen a grandson of Job's brother, was first cousin once removed to Catherine and not her second cousin).

Now it may be noticed that one twelfth of the estate remained unassigned: and this puzzled me a good deal at first. The explanation, I think, is that besides Ananiah and Thomas and their sister they had another brother or sister who either was not certainly known to be dead, or had left descendants either still alive or not proved to have died; and that the residual twelfth was left for his or her or their share. If I am right in suspecting that "brother John" was the father of the younger Zephaniah as well as of Ananiah and Thomas and the un-named daughter then the question arises whether this Zephaniah had married and left issue still alive, or not proved to have died.

One or two remarks may be made on the accounts. We may reasonably surmise that the large sum of cash in the house was actually the ready money in the bank, and that the "debts on bond" were not really debts but balances due to Job's banking clients. Since moreover the "debts on simple contract" included some expenses of administration, I suggest that such expenses were possibly the salaries of clerks occupied in collecting all the outstanding debts ledgered in No. 25. How those responsible contrived to spend £135 on the funeral, and what possible extravagance they can have perpetrated which would account for this enormous expenditure, I fail to understand. Job was buried in Lansallos churchyard, but to my great regret the inscription on his tomb has been allowed to decay utterly.

CORRIGENDA

Since the Raphiel Rentals were printed I have devoted some hours further study to them, the result of which is that sundry corrections must be made.

Most of the additional time spent on these Rentals was devoted to the attempt to unravel a mystery about No. 75, the history of which in subsequent years had already puzzled and worried me. Some hopeless muddle seems to have been made in 1800: and I finally came to the conclusion that either the data regarding two different houses – or tenements – had somehow been confused together, or that one house – or tenement – was divided into two in 1800. The evidence is that in all the later Rentals I find two tenements instead of the one described in 1800 as "late Lawrence Toms" – one retaining this description, leased to Richard Rowett (who was dead before 1806) at 3s 6d rent with no heriot on the lives of Phillis and John Rowett; and the other described as "late Rommett's" leased to Charles Rowett at 5s rent and 10s heriot on the lives of himself and his wife Martha and his daughter Susanna. This tenement I now number 75-A. The fact that no heriot was payable on the former is perhaps an argument for regarding this tenement as originally part of the latter house; and L. Toms' clearly was anyhow large enough to be divided into several tenements, as Nos. 72 and 78

– and perhaps Nos. 33 and 78? – were parts of it. Finally, as regards the intermarriage of Rommett and Rowett, the addition of "daur" to Phillis Rowett's name in the list suggests that she was Jane Rommett's daughter.

In the Rental of 1806 the Jane Barrett, who succeeded to No. 11, must have been Barrett's daughter; for the later-discovered list of heriots payable proves that his wife had died before 1800. Richard Rowett's executors are entered for No. 75; while No. 75-A is still held by Charles Rowett, who has also a "new house". I had omitted to note that the lives of David Thompson and Mary his wife are now entered in No. 85: but the ages are not given.

In the comments on the Rental of 1808 "Jonathan Barrett" and "Jonathan Rowett" were misreadings for "John". Next after No. 50 comes a new John Mark as tenant for No. 4 – now converted into "house on the quay" – on the original Baker lives. (I believe that the attached houses in which Messrs Thomas and John Mark now live are probably this No. 4.)

In the Rental of 1810 the description of No. 30 is altered to "two houses"; and "at Crumplehorn" is added.

————

ADDENDA

When I had nearly finished my task of writing all this story Messrs Job handed me yet another instalment – fortunately a small one – of odd papers that they had found. Among these were the covers of No. 11. These were labelled 1790:

but all the records of 1790, and most of those of 1791, remain missing. It was interesting to find, however, a few pages devoted to "barley sold at Looe" in 1791. There were also pages 59 to 178, some of these however missing, of what was clearly a book later than No. 11 and earlier than No. 12 which I have therefore labelled 11-A. The records are of purchases in the autumn of 1792 and in the spring and summer of 1793. The covers, of course, are missing.

There were also the following additions:

No. 2 – Accounts of the year 1794, previously missing.

No. 4-A – Pages 13 to 22 (1783 to 1786) of Job's accounts with Mrs Eastcott, which I have packed with No. 4 and labelled 4-A.

No. 7 – Several pages of 1791, which thus add another year to this volume.

No. 19 – Some tattered pages perhaps belonging to this "corpus vile"; but, on the re-examination this necessitated, some pages formerly assigned to No. 19, including at least some of the "writings", were transferred to No. 18, the earliest date of No. 19 is now perhaps 1802. (It may be worth mention that in No. 18 or 19 are some pages on which the expenses, at any rate, of Killiow Farm are tabulated).

No. 28 – A previously missing section from late July 1803 to Michaelmas, 1804.

No. 30 – Very damaged fragments of a subsidiary daybook, which may have belonged to the earlier part of this, and have now been put with it, though no date of year is left on any page. A small fragment of 1801, which probably formed part of this book, and some of the previously missing pages of 1804, have also been added.

About ten damaged pages of size 12¼ by 8 are the wreckage of some hitherto unknown account book ranging from 1816 or earlier to 1820. I have not assigned a number.

No. 43 – Some very tattered fragments of 1818 and 1819 were evidently torn from this book.

This latest find included also two more Rentals of Raphiel namely those for 1804 and 1807. I have looked through these, and compared them with those for 1806 and 1808: and fortunately it is unnecessary to comment on them.

* * * * *

As regards the lime-burner Mr C. K. C. Andrew writes me that "there was formerly a kiln or kilns about the site of the house called 'Tregertha' in Station-road, Looe". I do not know whether this can have been the site purchased by Job from Major Nicholas in 1803. Mr Andrew also quotes from a demise of Trenake in 1812, in which he noticed "that the stipulations as to husbandry called for forty customary bushels of well burnt stone lime or 100 horse-seams of good salt sea-sand per acre". No wonder that Job did such a tremendous trade in lime!

* * * * *

With regard to Job's accounts for the sales of pilchards to Leghorn and Naples, I have to thank Mr Andrew for the information that the unit at

Leghorn was the pezza or piastre, worth about forty-nine pence at par, and the Neapolitan unit the ducat, worth about forty or forty-one pence.

* * * * *

Mr Andrew has been able to add also one more example of Job's varied activities: for it seems that Job received £25 for taking the dung of East Looe during the year from 8th October, 1803, to 29th September, 1804.

* * * * *

To the story of Job's stewardships I must add that in 1805 his salary from Pooley was increased to five guineas; but that in 1803 his salary from Eastcott fell from thirty guineas to ten.

* * * * *

At the end of these Gleanings I wish to repeat my acknowledgements to Messrs Job, who have not only given me free access to the records but have been so good as to leave the collection in my charge for a twelvemonth. I wish also to emphasise once more the importance of securing all such records for some public library or museum, where they would be carefully preserved and made available for the use of students. I suspect that Messrs Job would be far from willing to part with these relics of their great-great-uncle; but it is very much to be desired that the authorities of some public library in the West Country should be able to come to an arrangement with them for the public good. Meantime, for my own part, I thank them very heartily.

ALPHABETICAL LIST OF SURNAMES OCCURRING IN THE FOREGOING RECORDS.

In dealing with the surnames in these records I was faced with certain difficulties that had not occurred in my study of the records of Talland and Lansallos parishes. In those former cases it was important and practicable to note every surname – for reasons already explained in "The Records of Lansallos", but in dealing with the Job records the conditions were so different that the following list is not comparable with those of Talland and Lansallos, and for these reasons.

(1) Since these records are contemporary with parts of those in Talland and Lansallos, there could be no object in listing surnames already noted merely for the sake of making a complete list.

(2) On the other hand, numbers of names already recorded for Talland and for Lansallos occur in the following list, because they have necessarily been quoted in the foregoing pages.

(3) When I noticed names not previously recorded for Talland or Lansallos, I listed these for the sake of recording them even when there was otherwise nothing whatever to say about the holders of the names: but it would be strange if some names have not escaped me when the records are so voluminous.

(4) As already explained, I have ignored entirely the surnames in No. 1 and very many in No. 6, and I have similarly ignored nearly all those in Nos. 9-15 which seem to belong to other parishes than Talland and Lansallos,

besides the names in the volumes asterisked (*) in the Catalogue. Some other student might reap a biggish harvest here. Contrariwise some names certainly belonging to other parishes are listed below because they were borne by men whose doings came into my story.

Finally, as the names of various folk in Guernsey and London and elsewhere have been necessarily quoted, I have listed these separately.

LOCAL NAMES

(Those marked * are suspected or believed or known to have been not native to Talland or Lansallos.)

A'Lee
{Algar
{Alger
Allen
Andrew
{Aunger
{Angear
Avery
Baker
Ball
Barrett
Bartlett
Bastard (Polruan)
Bate
{Batten
{Batting
*Bedford
Beer
Bellamy
Bennett
Bettinson
Billing
Bluett (St. Allens)
Bolling (Pelynt)
Botting
Bowden
Braddon
Broughton
*Brown
Buckthast
Buller
Bunt
Burn

Callaway
*Camelford, Lord
Carpenter (Devon)
Chark (e)
Clements
Clogg
Coad
Coath
*?Cock
Coles
{Collins
{Collings
Colman
Commerell (Fowey?)
Congdon
Conning
Cook
Cory
{Cortis
{Courtice
{Courtis
{Curtis
Cossentine
Couch
Cowling
{Cragoe
{Cragee
Croft
*?Dillon
Dingle
Donnithorne
Douster (?)
Draper

*?Dun
Dyer
Eastcott
Ede
Edwards
Ellis
Evea
{Fiddock
{Fiddick
Forward
Fowler
Frances (?)
Gambrell (Plymouth?)
Geach
Geake
George
Giddy
Gilbert
Gill
Goyen (St. Agnes?)
*Grantly, Lord
*Granville, Lord
Greet
Griffith(s)
Grigg
Guy
Hambly
Harding
Harris
{Hawken
{Hawkin
{Heal
{Hele
Hearle
Henna
Hickey
Hicks
{Higgens
{Higgins

Hill
Hitchens
Hobb
{Hocken
{Hockin(s)
{Hocking
Hodge
*Holdsworth
{Hoil
{Hole
{Holten
{Holton
{Holting
Honey
Hooper
Hore
Hoskin
{Houghton
{Hoyton
{Hutton
Howell
Jago
James
Jasper
Jeffery
{Jenkings (St. Mawes)
{Jenkins (St. Mawes)
Job
Johns
Jose
Kean (St. Austell)
Keast
Kendall
*Lake
{Langmaid
{Langmead
Leach
Lean
Leatherby

Ledstone   {Pearn
Lego   Parsons
{Libbey   {Pascho
{Libby   {Pascoe
Lightfoot   Peake
Little (Morval)   {Pearce
Littleton   {Pearse
Luke   Perkin
Lukey   Perry
Mark(s)   Peters
Martin(g)   Phillipps
May   Phillis
{Maynard   {Pinsent
{Minard(s)   {Pincent
Mayow(e) (Bray)   Pinch
Medland   Pine
Meggs   Pitt (Boconnoc)
Mellow   Polgrain
Menear   Pollard
*Millett   *Pomery
*?Mills   Pooley
Mitchell   *?Potter
Molesworth (Egloshayle)   Powne
{Monford   Pryer (Polruan)
{Monkford   Puckey
Moore   Puddicombe
Morshead   Quiller
*Moysey (where?)   Rabby
Mutton   Rashleigh
*Naptune   {Rain
Nicholas   {Rean
Nicholls   Rawling
Northcott   *Rawlings
Notwell   {Rundle
Oliver   {Rendle
Ough   Rice
Pachyn   Richards
Parkin   Rickard
{Parne   Roberts

Robins
{Rommett
{Rummett
Roose
Roskilly
Rowe
Rowett
Sargent
Salusbury
Sawle
Searle
Shapcott
*Shipman
Skinner
Slade
Sleeman
Snell
Soady
Solomon
Spershott
Stap
Steed
{Stephens
{Stephings
{*?Stevens
Stivey
Stocker (Fowey)
*Stone (where?)
Styart
Swartman
{Taprill
{Taprell
Teague
Thomas
Thompson
Tinney
Toms
Tonkin (St. Agnes)
Tozer

{Tregair(e)
{Tregare
Trehane
Trelawny
Truscott
Tucker (?)
Turner
Vague
{Vandersluce
{*Vanderslys
{Vandersluys
Venton
*Vigurs
Wakeham
Walsh
Walton
Wareham
Warren
Warne
*Webb
Whetter
Whipple (Polruan)
{Willcock
{Wilcock
Williams
Wills
*?Wilson
Wise
Wyatt
Wynhall

Aubin (London but †)
Boucault (Guernsey)
Brock (Guernsey and London)
de Carteret (Guernsey)
Clough (London)
Combes (Guernsey)
Cammerell (London)
Corbin (Guernsey)
Dobrel (London but presumably but †)
Dodd (London)
Downing (Ireland)
Ferdinandis (Portugal?)
Glass (London)
Goldsmith (London)
Guille (Guernsey)
Hillary (Guernsey)
Huddart (Leghorn)
de Jersey (Guernsey and London)
Lange (London)
Lemesurier (London but †)
Laseere (Guernsey)
de Lisle (Guernsey)
Lubbock (London)
Lukis (Guernsey)
Maingy (Guernsey)
Moullin (Guernsey)
Mourant (Guernsey)
Nicholas (Naples)
Parr (London)
Payton (London?)
Perchard (London but †)
Plummer (Oxford)
Porter (Leghorn)
Priaulx (Guernsey)
Robbilliard (Alderney)
Smith (London)
Stripling (Leghorn)
Thomme (Guernsey)
(Names marked † are obviously of Guernsey or
Jersey origin.)